# A WEDDING FOR ALL SEASONS

# A WEDDING FOR ALL SEASONS

Bette Matthews

FRIEDMAN/FAIRFAX

A FRIEDMAN/FAIRFAX BOOK

© 2002 by Michael Friedman Publishing Group, Inc.

Please visit our website: www.metrobooks.com

Library of Congress Cataloging-in-Publication Data

Matthews, Bette.
    A Wedding for all seasons / Bette Matthews.
        p.cm.
    Includes bibliographical references and index.
    ISBN 1-58663-077-6 (alk. paper)
    1. Weddings—Planning. 2. Seasons. I. Title.

HQ745 .M3248 2002
395.2′2--dc21

                                        2001040610

Editors: Ann Kirby-Payne and Rosy Ngo
Art Director: Jeff Batzli
Designer: Kirsten Berger
Photography Editor: Lori Epstein
Production Manager: Richela Fabian-Morgan

Color separations by Fine Arts Repro House Co., Ltd
Printed in Italy by Milanostampa

1  3  5  7  9  10  8  6  4  2

Distributed by Sterling Publishing Company, Inc.
387 Park Avenue South
New York, NY 10016
Distributed in Canada by Sterling Publishing
Canadian Manda Group
One Atlantic Avenue, Suite 105
Toronto, Ontario, Canada M6K 3E7
Distributed in Australia by
Capricorn Link (Australia) Pty, Ltd.
P.O. Box 704, Windsor, NSW 2756 Australia

# Acknowledgments

I owe my greatest gratitude, appreciation, and love to my husband, Antonio, who not only stood by me through the entire process of writing this book, but contributed his own talents to this project by way of his beautiful photographs. Working together through many days of shooting taught me a greater appreciation of his art and his eye. Although he doesn't share my passion for weddings, he expertly translated ideas into lasting impressions, and having so many of his photographs in this book makes it particularly meaningful to me.

Many, many thanks go to the publishing staff at Friedman/Fairfax. To former editorial director Sharyn Rosart and editor-extraordinaire Ann Kirby-Payne, my appreciation for offering me the opportunity to translate the vision for this book into words. Special thanks to Ann as well for her fortitude, serenity, and gentle editor's pen. To my new editor Rosy Ngo, my gratitude for her encouragement, enthusiasm, and level-headed sensibility. Thanks also to Chris Bain for offering this photographer/author husband-and-wife team the opportunity to translate words into photographs. I'm grateful to Lori Epstein for her tireless efforts to locate the exceptional photographs that fill these pages, as well as for her wonderful photographic judgment. I'd also like to thank designer Kirsten Berger for her talented work on this project (and the previous books as well). Thanks also to Hallie Einhorn and Melissa McKoy for their help at the Central Park Boathouse shoot.

Finally, I am greatly indebted to the people and companies who offered their time, skills, and contributions to help breathe life into my ideas. Thanks to Jennifer Spell for her generosity in stepping in to assist with the photo shoot at the Central Park Boathouse. My sincere appreciation to Linda Lieberman of TriServe Party Rentals and Just Linens, for the tremendous amount of time and energy she gave to this project, for her suggestions as well as for her impeccable taste, and to Beth Parle for her patience and hard work each time she stepped up to the plate. To floral designers Elizabeth Ryan, Jennifer Pfeiffer of Magnolia, and Lisa McWilliams, for bringing nature's best to our tables, my thanks and admiration for their abilities. To Donna Scaramucci and chef Alan Ashkenaze of the Boathouse in Central Park, I'm grateful for the opportunity to work in such an incredible space and sample such delectable dishes. Thanks as well to Michael Davis at the Cloth Connection for his generous contributions to our tables. To Peter Callahan of Callahan Catering and chef Beth Parker, for a delightful (and delicious) day of shooting, my esteem and gratitude. Warmest thanks to calligraphers Angela Welch, Stephannie Barba, Susan Ramsey, and Hilary Williams for their exquisite work. Thanks to Tara and the staff at the Clay Pot for their assistance and their trust. Finally, to Meiers Tambeau, Arora Beattie, and Cally Guasti for lending me some essential props from their personal collections, my appreciation and hugs.

# Contents

# Introduction

June is, most certainly, the month most typically linked to being wed. But pick a day—any day of the year—and you can bet that someone, somewhere, is planning to be married then. Weddings are a year-round occurrence and a cause for celebration whenever they take place.

Today's bride and groom are not limited by seasonal scarcities; in fact, finding inspiration in each season opens up limitless possibilities for personalizing this most joyous of rituals. Taking a cue from Mother Nature herself, the wedding planner (be it a hired consultant, a creative family member, or the well-organized bride) will find boundless opportunity for flavoring the event with savory details that are abundant during, or appropriate to, a particular time of year.

"Details" is the word of the day when it comes to planning a wedding. From the moment a couple gets engaged, they are inundated with decisions concerning their nuptials. And while the institution of marriage may seem a trifle old-fashioned, today's bride and groom have the option to set a traditional or unconventional tone—or something in between. If this all seems overwhelming, take heart. Think of your wedding as you would any other project…with a beginning, a middle, and an end. Once each step is broken down into manageable chores, develop a vision for the big picture, and take each step one at a time.

If you're not considering eloping (or even if you are), read on. This book will walk you through many of the phases common to planning every wedding, from ceremony to soirée, clothing to cakes. And with each step, you'll get a glimpse of how to put your personal stamp on the festivities.

Keep your eye on the special conditions and unique opportunities presented by the specific time of year during which you plan to have your wedding. With equal parts organization, imitation, and imagination, you will create a beautiful and memorable wedding in any of the four seasons.

ABOVE: *A traditional approach to the wedding program is always elegant. A simple, folded card, with the program set in a classic script, and printed on fine paper, can be adorned with a satin cord and tassel.*

OPPOSITE: *If your ceremony or reception location doesn't have any outdoor space available, plan enough time for a detour. Public parks and botanical gardens provide beautiful backdrops for your formal photographs. Be sure to check with the facility to find out if there are any restrictions.*

## Chapter One

# To Everything There Is a Season

ABOVE: *Delightful daisies add an extra bit of panache and fortify the white-on-white color scheme for the day.*

OPPOSITE: *A trainless dress is a good choice when the weather might be wet. This tulle-skirted ball gown is hemmed so it won't drag through puddles. A spare pair of shoes might help until you get to your destination, and a casual wrap will prepare you for any outdoor photo opportunities.*

We've heard that March comes in like a lion and goes out like a lamb, and that April showers bring May flowers. When we think of July, we think of fireworks and watermelon and swimming on hot days, while September means back to school. October is wrapped in brilliant colors of red and orange and gold, and November smells like pumpkin pie. January is white as far as the eye can see. Even if we don't actually live in a climate that changes dramatically from season to season, these images are a part of our shared culture and come instantly to mind when asked to capture a season in words. Choosing a seasonal approach will make the planning process easier, as there is inspiration in the natural world around you.

The first question many newly engaged couples are asked is "Have you set the date?" Finding the answer to that question comes with a different set of criteria for each duo. Some choose a wedding date after laborious debate, carefully considering every aspect and weighing the consequences. Does it interfere with anyone's vacation schedule? Will your favorite nephew be home from college? Is the date on a holiday weekend, and is that an inconvenience or a blessing? Others choose a time with sentiment attached to it, and no further thought is necessary; the anniversary of your first date, your mom's birthday, or Christmastime (because that is when you got engaged) may seem like the perfect time for your celebration. Still others have their dates thrust upon them by necessity; trying to schedule a wedding when someone is on leave from military service, fitting it in after finals and before your summer internship starts, or discovering that there is only one Saturday during which both your ceremony site and your reception hall are available, you may be required to conform to a timetable other than your own. Finally, there are those people who have always envisioned getting married at a certain time of year—their favorite season.

# A Year in the Life

## Summer: June, July, August

Forever linked with the idea of vacation, summer is the time to kick back and relax. The earth is green everywhere you look, and flowers are in full bloom. Swimming during the day, watching fireflies at night, napping in a hammock in the shade of your favorite tree—these lazy days of summer are glorious. Use summer's charm by planning a picnic, barbecue, or beach wedding. Illuminate the night with tiki torches or paper lanterns. Give a nod to Independence Day with your own fireworks display, or use sparklers as a send-off instead of birdseed or rose petals. Bright colors will fit right in, as will perky pastel ginghams or earth-toned awning stripes. Serve pitchers of lemonade, invite guests to go barefoot, and make your getaway in a convertible or motorboat.

## Autumn: September, October, November

Mother Nature treats us to a riot of color as she leaves summer behind. Back to school and back to work, it's time to get serious and settle into a new schedule. That doesn't mean you should forget about fun, because this is the season of barn dances, carved pumpkins, and big, welcoming feasts. The harvest brings its wealth to your table, and an overflowing cornucopia is an appropriate symbol of this bounty. Perfume the room with hot apple cider. Use vegetables, fruits, gourds, and trailing ivy to decorate tables. Mimic nature's deep colors of red, gold, burgundy, and rust, and add texture to your fabrics. Allow your playful side to peek through, giving a nod to your favorite holiday by dressing your bridesmaids in black and choosing orange flowers for their bouquets.

## Winter: December, January, February

The holiday season is in full bloom. Christmas, Hanukkah, and Kwanzaa get the spirit going. New Year's Eve and the Chinese New Year are not far behind, and Valentine's Day brings up the rear. Everywhere you go, the world seems dressed for a party, and that may mean you have less decorating to do for your ceremony or reception site. Jewel tones, dark colors, and touches of gold and silver are common, and don't forget about winter white. Frosty accents like crystals and delicate snowflakes materialize in astounding shapes. The heart, of course, is the perfect symbol. Candles and fairy lights add sparkle and magic to your wedding. Use a wreath on the door to bid your guests welcome or on the table to encircle a centerpiece. Provide an evergreen tree to replace the gift table and ask each guest to bring an ornament to decorate it.

## Spring: March, April, May

The earth renews itself and everyone shakes off the chill of winter. There is a hopefulness about everything as the first spring flowers push themselves into view. Butterflies flit about, and the chirping of birds fills the morning air. In the springtime, let the sun shine in. Flowering plants and bulbs create stunning centerpieces that can break apart for favors at the end of the event. Pastel colors abound, but bolder hues are just as effective. Wispy fabrics add airiness and light to garments and linens. Paint your guests' names and table numbers on Easter eggs instead of place cards. This is the time of Mardi Gras and Carnivale, so serve king cake for your groom's cake and send your guests home with feathered masks or strings of beads as favors. Whatever you do, don't wear green to a wedding on St. Patrick's Day, as it's considered bad luck.

So how do you choose? For the purpose of this book, each month has been linked to a particular season. Incorporating the elements that are plentiful at the time will seem a natural fit and save money. On the other hand, there are no rules, so use your instincts to freely mix and match your favorite details at any time of year. Talk it over with your fiancé and your families. Be flexible and open to change. Each season brings its own grand pageantry, with rich images from that time of year. Of course, each season also brings its own challenges to the process of planning a wedding.

*Above: A wreath of summery blooms encircles a romantic lantern. Even during the daytime, a citronella candle is useful at an outdoor wedding to ward off insects.*

## Fooling with Mother Nature

No matter what the season, there will be natural obstacles to overcome in order to enjoy an idyllic wedding. Here are tips for making the most of your wedding any time of year.

## SUMMER

Keep your guests' comfort (as well as your own) in mind as you plan your summer wedding. Of course, an air-conditioned room will keep everyone fresh as a daisy, but good ventilation and powerful fans can also be effective. Hot, sunny days are delightful for an outdoor wedding, but you *can* have too much of a good thing. If parts of the ceremony or reception will take place outdoors, take advantage of nature's own umbrellas and set up your ceremony under a canopy of trees. A backup plan is always wise: a tent can provide a shady respite or be a haven in inclement weather. If little shade or limited seating is available, reserve it for the youngest and more senior members of the guest list, as they will be most susceptible to the sun's effects.

Insects are a pesky problem during summertime. Be sure that windows are screened. Mosquitoes can be relentless prior to or just after a storm. Have a professional exterminator spray outside areas as close to the start of the event as is practical. Citronella candles are perfect for the summer wedding, providing a natural insect repellent as well as an option for lighting.

*Suggestions for Summer*

- Pretty parasols or white umbrellas can help make guests more comfortable, providing shade from the sun or protection from the rain.

- Have plenty of nonalcoholic drinks available from the moment guests arrive to ward off dehydration. Set up a bar of "designer" spring and sparkling waters.

- Provide cans of insect repellent at an outdoor event so that guests are not distracted by mosquitoes, and keep a first-aid kit available with treatments for bites or stings.

## AUTUMN

This is a time of change, and the ability to go with the flow will carry you a long way for an autumn wedding. Early in the season, the temperature can be unpredictable, making decisions about your wedding attire tricky. Choose garments that will be appropriate, whether it's Indian summer or a bit on the nippy side. This is a great opportunity when dressing in layers of clothing—a wrap, a scarf, or a sweater—will keep you comfortable no matter which way the temperature goes. Colorful foliage provides a brilliant backdrop for outdoor photos, but falling leaves can be very slippery, so be sure that all walkways are carefully cleared.

The change of the clocks comes with the change of the seasons, and darkness falls earlier and earlier as the weeks progress. Planning a reception in the countryside allows you to enjoy the full effect of autumn's attraction. But remember a daytime wedding may end in darkness. Consider your guests' safety as they enter and leave the event, making sure all areas are well lit. And whatever you do, avoid a honeymoon destination that will be in the throws of hurricane season!

### *Autumnal Advice*

- Treat yourself and your bridesmaids to luxurious pashmina wraps and you'll look forward to a chill in the air.

- Light a path with carved pumpkins lined up on either side that radiate with the glow of votive candles.

- Make your wedding into a weekend-long event. Host the reception at a country bed-and-breakfast and arrange a discounted room rate, so your guests don't have to travel after the party ends.

ABOVE: *Small details lend a pinch of seasonal charm. A gourd set atop an arrangement of skeleton leaves adds a splash of color to each place setting.*

## WINTER

As the old year comes to an end and the new one gets under way, everyone is already in a celebratory mood, but guests' social obligations can conflict with your arrangements. Send "save the date" cards out about six months before the wedding to alert guests to your plans so that appropriate travel and lodging arrangements can be made. Tourist season in some areas will mean difficulty arranging last minute hotel rooms.

Lack of daylight and foul weather could make travel more difficult and sometimes even dangerous. Leave yourself plenty of time to reach your destinations and make sure vehicles are in tip-top shape. Plan your ceremony and reception in close proximity of one another to avoid excessive travel, and consider starting the festivities on the early side. Be sure there are sufficient accommodations for coats and umbrellas. Flowers can get very pricey at holiday times. The cost of roses skyrockets around Valentine's Day, and their availability plummets. Ask your floral designer if this will be an issue, and discuss possible alternatives.

### Winter Wisdom

- Take advantage of all that darkness and light up the night with candles. A candlelight ceremony, followed by a reception enhanced by the glow of dancing wicks, will warm up a frosty evening.

- Provide a shuttle bus to transport guests from ceremony to reception (and, of course, back again at the end of the celebration).

- Greet guests with a hot drink or cocktail to instantly quell the chill of winter.

## SPRING

Cabin fever subsides and everyone's spirits lift. The earth prepares itself for a new phase of life, just as you do. With all that growth comes the dreaded allergy season, and there's little you can do to alleviate that particular brand of distress. If you or your groom suffers at this time of year, you may want to push the date back a bit. Be prepared for rain, rain, and more rain. Ask if your ceremony location has a room you can use to change into your bridal attire. Ongoing rain means soggy ground, so protect your shoes against mud. And if gray skies bring your spirits down, try to remember that without the rain, you wouldn't be holding that beautiful bouquet of flowers—Mother Nature is charmingly cyclical that way.

Of course, as the clocks spring ahead, confusion sets in. If your wedding date coincides with that particular weekend, remind your parents, wedding party, and vendors of the time change—and prepare to lose an hour's sleep or preparation time. It's far better to be thought overly cautious than to discover someone is missing in action at the wedding itself. That advice applies to you as well. There's nothing more disappointing than starting your honeymoon by arriving at the airport to discover that your plane has just left.

### Spring Sense

- For the ceremony, provide little packets of tissues wrapped in ribbon for both allergy sufferers and your most sentimental guests.
- Take advantage of that extra hour of daylight by planning a midday home wedding and let the party run its natural course throughout the day.

ABOVE: *Don't let it rain on your parade. Even inclement weather can become an opportunity for fond memories—with a little help from your friends.*

## Chapter Two

# In the Beginning...

ABOVE: *There are many creative options for informal wedding stationery. This couple combined a play on words from a favorite movie title with an origami technique for their clever invitation.*

OPPOSITE: *Roses are always in season. Here, they are mixed with sweet peas to form a beautiful focal point that calls attention to the French doors leading to a sunny veranda.*

Your wedding date is set, or at least you have a range of dates in mind, and now you are ready to begin planning and organizing this momentous event. You'll find this to be a juggling act—with many of the parts somewhat interchangeable. But you have to start somewhere, so the first basic decisions to tackle are budget and style. Discuss how much you can afford to spend on this event with each other and with your parents. Keep in mind that the style and location of the event will directly influence the cost. Formal events often (though not always) are more expensive than informal affairs, and urban areas tend to be pricey. Your ideas will emerge as you talk them over and start your research. It is likely that both budget and style may metamorphose as you begin to speak with vendors and get a sense of exactly what you want. But once you're armed with a general knowledge of what you can spend and what you'd like to spend it on, you're ready to venture forth.

Tackle the biggest issues first: choosing a location for your ceremony and reception. If these two critical parts of your wedding will not be held in the same place, coordinating both for the same day is the prime directive. You may desire to be wed at a familiar house of worship, and that would be the place to start confirming dates. Or perhaps your heart is set on a reception hall in another area, and you will have to locate a suitable spot for the ceremony. The less travel time between ceremony and reception, the better. Remember that holiday schedules fill up quickly, with many people and organizations planning activities, so if your wedding coincides with a holiday, get started as early as possible. Be flexible. Keep each of the locations informed of your progress in firming up the arrangements with the other, and don't dawdle over your decision.

If the reception hall does not have an onsite caterer, finding one should be your next order of business—although sometimes a caterer, or any other vendor, can steer you toward some interesting sites where they have worked. You'll have a whirlwind of interviews and tastings ahead of you before you finalize your menu. This is often one of the groom's favorite parts! There will be so much excitement in the days ahead. Savor each moment and each activity, and then move on to the next one.

## A Beautiful Site

Choosing a location is a matter of personal preference. Although some reception sites lend themselves to many styles, others dictate a certain level of formality—or lack thereof. Each site will have its own essence. A hotel wedding can be very grand. It is usually held in a ballroom, where the wide-open space, high ceiling, and stately decor suggest a formal approach. Wonderful at any time of year, an elegant hotel wedding is particularly advantageous in the winter months, when travel can be difficult. A block of rooms can be reserved for your guests, usually at discounted rates, making it convenient for them to extend the celebration to the next day and then journey home in daylight. A loft has

similar spaciousness and is frequently decorated more sparingly, allowing your imagination

to take over and fill in the space with seasonal details. Many historic sites are available

for rental and can vary greatly in style. A dignified mansion may be the perfect choice

for a chilly autumn or winter day, when a roaring fire in the marble fireplace will really

set the mood. A charming barn is the perfect locale for an autumn gala, complete with

pumpkin centerpieces and bales of hay in lieu of ceremony chairs. A cheerful hall with

floor-to-ceiling windows set in the middle of your local park is fabulous in every season,

but especially gorgeous when the park is lush and green in summer or afire with the

colors of fall. A restaurant wedding will take on the flavor of the venue, where the chef

# The Tent Wedding

Appropriate at almost any time of year, the tent wedding is steeped in romance. It can be as formal or as casual as you wish, and it offers the perfect opportunity for putting panache into your wedding plans.

Practically speaking, you won't want to pitch your tent at the height of a snowy winter season, but air conditioning and heating can be added to make it comfortable at any other time of year. If electricity is not available, a generator will provide all the energy necessary for lighting, temperature control, and ventilation. Of course, your musicians and caterers will also need power. Your tent should have sidewalls that roll up during good weather. The flaps can be solid, have windows or doors, or be completely clear. You can even order a clear roof or one with skylights, although these options are better for nighttime stargazing than for broiling under the midday sun. Consider screening or bug netting to keep out insects. Add flooring to the full dimension of the tent, use a dance floor only, or skip flooring altogether to create a more casual atmosphere. But be aware that bare ground will present some setbacks: high heels have a tendency to dig into the grass, and in heavy rain, the earth gets very wet and muddy, especially around the edges of the tent.

A series of connecting tents or canopies is an excellent idea and creates different environments for your guests. The caterer will need a place to work, of course, and that area can be connected to a food presentation tent, if you are having a buffet, or directly to the main tent. A separate bar tent can be outfitted as a place to gather and chat or as a smoking area apart from the central room. Perhaps you'll want your cake to have its own pavilion, or you'll want to set up an independent area for dancing. Whatever may be your dreams, tents offer the flexibility to design a completely original wedding.

When it comes to decorating, the tent is a blank canvas for you to adorn in any way you see fit. The ceiling can be wired for elegant chandeliers or colorful paper lanterns. Add uplights for dramatic impact. Drape the walls in yard after yard of shirred fabric overlaying thousands of tiny fairy lights. Turn the tent poles into seasonal focal points by covering them in moss or flowers, surrounding them with corn- or wheat stalks, or wrapping them in fabric and autumn leaves. Decorate the tent's entrance with baskets of flowering plants or wreaths of seasonal blossoms. When working with multiple tents, it's fun to decorate each a little differently, distinguishing them from one another, so that each "room" has its own character. Don't let them get too disjointed, however: tie them together with a similar concept or palette to show that they still have a relationship.

Chances are that you will have to make arrangements for portable lavatories at this type of event, and you will be amazed at how comfortable these restrooms can be. Equipped with lighting, mirrors, sinks, and the latest sanitation facilities, they have space for scented candles, potpourri, and extra supplies. Make arrangements to have someone attend the restrooms to keep them clean and well stocked. It's good to have an assortment of umbrellas near the tent entrance in case of inclement weather, and make sure the path to and from the bathrooms is well lit at an evening event. The rental facility will have sanitation guidelines based on the attendance and duration of your reception to help with these accommodations.

is already adept at creating sumptuous menus from the bounty of the season.

For many, getting married outdoors is a dream come true. Weather permitting, there is something especially romantic about exchanging vows under sun or stars, but be sure to have a backup plan. Consider local parks and sites with gardens, pools, or decks. Or, as Dorothy learned, your heart's desire may lie no farther than your own backyard (or that of your future in-laws'). A home wedding has an intimacy unmatched by any other location.

ABOVE: *There's no place like home. A rented tent, tableware, and chairs can turn a backyard into the most private of reception halls. If the weather is uncooperative, flaps can be added to the tent's sides to create a dry haven.*

## Finding a Location

Start by making a list of reception sites in your area. Depending on where you live, you may have a wide assortment of places to choose from, or your options may be limited. Ask for recommendations from family and friends. Your church or synagogue might have some suggestions as well. In fact, some even have community rooms for rent.

The Yellow Pages is a great tool for all your wedding research. You'll find listings under "Wedding Supplies and Services," "Banquet Facilities," "Caterers," and "Halls & Auditoriums," as well as restaurants, hotels and inns, country clubs and other clubs, and museums. If you live near the water, there may be yachts available for large events as well. The local chamber of commerce is a good resource, as is your city's bureau of tourism. Consultants, event planners, offsite caterers, and other wedding vendors will be able to recommend locations they are familiar with, so make initial contact early in your search. Call the historic preservation societies for suggestions of historic sites available for rental. Check out your local park or botanical garden: these often have historic buildings or community rooms available for rent or will allow, with proper permits, a tented event to be scheduled.

There are many wedding magazines published with regional listings, although these concentrate mostly on urban areas. While rare, wedding announcements in newspapers occasionally list the location of the reception, but a better source might be the society pages. These days, just about everyone has a website, and an Internet search will certainly provide some leads. There are also many wedding chat boards, with participants from all over the country (as well as other countries) who are happy to offer advice and suggestions.

## WHAT TO LOOK FOR

With list in hand, begin your research on the telephone. The banquet manager or event coordinator of the location you choose will be able to answer basic questions and set up an appointment for you to see the space. It is important to develop a good rapport with this person, who will be your main contact for the event. You'll want to feel that this person will address all of your concerns, that your questions will be answered clearly, and that you have someone who cares about working with you to create an event that will run smoothly and bring your dream to life. Here's a checklist of things to consider.

ABOVE: *Whatever the weather, a breathtaking glass-ceilinged conservatory brings in the outdoors. Set in the midst of this city's botanical gardens, the inside of this party space is as dazzling as its surroundings. Decorative lights intermingle with more practical illumination to highlight the spectacular ceiling and mimic the stars in the night sky.*

**Date and time:** Is the room available on the date or dates you have selected? How far in advance can you reserve the room? How long can a date be held open for you while you make your decision? How many hours are included for the event itself, and what is the policy regarding setup time? Does your party have to end at its scheduled hour, or can it run overtime?

**Size:** What is the room's capacity? Is the space big enough to accommodate all of your guests? Is it a larger space than you need, and is there any way to make it seem more intimate? Is there a place for the ceremony if you wish to have it in the same location? Is there a separate room for the cocktail hour? Is the dance floor big enough? Will other events be taking place at the same time as yours?

**Parking:** Is there valet parking? Is there enough parking available onsite? If not, is there adequate public parking nearby? If the answer to these questions is "No," consider making arrangements with a parking garage and having a shuttle bus transport your guests to and from their cars.

**Amenities:** Are there adequate bathroom facilities, and is an attendant assigned to keep them fresh and clean during the event? Will there be a coat check, and how many staff members will attend to it during the crunch times?

**Catering:** Is there an onsite caterer? If not, can the hall provide a list of approved caterers for you to choose from? Do you have the option of using someone different, and is there an approval process? Can you choose between a buffet or plated meal, and are there other types of catered receptions?

**Rentals:** Will they provide everything you need, or will you have to rent some items— from tables and chairs to linens and stemware?

**Restrictions:** Historic buildings often have restrictions on decorations, parking, and even music. Are there any restrictions that will interfere with your plans?

ABOVE: *An historic building has its own sense of dignity. Here, the dramatic lighting in an inner hallway creates contrast to the sun-bathed reception hall.*

**Price:** Per person, what's included? Is there a separate location fee or other additional fees? If the party runs overtime, what are the charges? Is liquor included in the cost, and if not, what are the charges? Are there any guarantees required for a minimum number of guests? How much must be paid in advance as a deposit (usually between 10 and 25 percent), and what is the payment schedule for the balance?

**References:** It's a wise precaution to speak with other people who have held events at this location to be certain that they were satisfied with the services. Ask for at least three references from recent events.

## ASSESS THE ROOM

Try to see the location at the same time of day as your reception so that you can assess the lighting and ambience. Before you make your final decision, look at the space during a similar event of comparable size.

**Decor:** Do you like the entrance? Is the color of the walls, carpet, or flooring pleasing, and does it work with your vision? How is the space decorated? Is there anything

## Put It in Writing

When you feel certain that you have found the location of your dreams and are ready to make a firm commitment, get it all on paper. A contract is a legal document that outlines expectations and protects both of you, should any glitches arise. It should include everything you discussed:

- name of the contact person who will be present on the day of the event
- date, time, length, and exact location (including the name of the room, if applicable)
- services rendered item by item, including a summary of the menu (if the menu has not been finalized yet, outline basically

what you will have) and bar arrangements (identifying the type and quality of beer, wine, and liquor served)

- equipment included (tables, chairs, linens, serving pieces, lighting, etc.)
- number of staff members and how they will be dressed
- minimum or maximum number of guests
- any promises made regarding renovations or decorating scheduled to take place prior to the event
- breakdown of fees, including the cancellation policy
- amount of deposit, date by which it is due, and payment schedule for balance

special, a feature that you love (or hate)? Remember that the space will look different when dressed up and lit for your wedding reception.

**Lighting and electricity:** If you are having a daytime event, are there windows? What is the view like? Is the lighting adequate and adjustable? Are open-flame candles or hurricane lanterns permitted? Are there enough outlets for other decorative lights, such as fairy lights or uplights, as well as outlets for the disc jockey or band?

**Space:** Is there any outdoor space available (depending on time of year)? Is the indoor space airy or cozy? Does the temperature feel comfortable and is there good ventilation? Will there be any obstructions to your guests' view? Is there one big room for the seated dinner, or will your guests be seated in several dining areas?

ABOVE: *An ornate ballroom establishes a formal setting. Tall centerpieces help to create a bridge in the vast space between the table and the ceiling; just make sure that they have slender bases to afford guests unobstructed views of each other.*

## The Movable Feast

If your location doesn't have an onsite catering staff, you will need to hire an independent caterer. This choice is critical to the success of your event, for even if you are not a "foodie," the quality of the food and the professionalism of the staff can make or break a party. The caterer often sets the pace of the celebration with the flow of food service and must be experienced enough to be able to read the crowd. The staff should be

courteous and helpful, placing the comfort of your guests at top priority; the staff should also be equipped to deal with any unexpected incidents or emergencies. You are truly putting your money where your mouth is: your catering costs can add up to 50 percent of the total bill, so be certain that your money is well spent.

Start with an initial round of telephone interviews. If the representative is not able to give you full attention at the moment, he or she should courteously suggest another time to talk. If someone is unwilling to find time for you in the beginning, when trying to woo your business, chances are you'll find that person to be unresponsive later on. Begin your conversation by checking the availability of the date you have in mind. Be prepared to provide an estimate of the number of guests expected (even though this may change as your planning progresses), and find out if you will have to guarantee a minimum number of guests when you go to contract. A final head count is usually not needed until one or two weeks before the wedding. Discuss your ideas about the type of meal, the style of the wedding, and any specific concepts or foods you want to have. Can they handle any unusual food service you might be planning, such as a barbecue or hors

LEFT: *This catering hall's staff stands at attention as the guests arrive. Available to assist with seating arrangements and any other immediate needs, they will also fill the wineglass of each guest as he or she sits down.*

# Check Please!

Catering costs can sometimes be negotiated, based on the type of meal you wish to serve. If you're looking to cut costs, don't plan on serving dishes made with costly ingredients, such as caviar or fresh truffles. Consider a brunch or luncheon, an hors d'oeuvre reception, or a dessert reception as an alternative to a full-course dinner. Some caterers charge less for a buffet meal because there is less work needed than in preparing and presenting individual plates. Others charge less for plated meals because more food is needed and many extra serving pieces are used with a buffet. Many make no distinction between the two and charge a flat rate regardless of what you serve, so if you are undecided about this issue, ask questions.

Meals are charged per person, so a larger guest list means higher costs. You should be charged less for children's meals and vendor meals (yes, you have to feed your wedding professionals, such as the band and the photographer, but the caterer should be responsible for their own staff). For an offsite caterer, the number of waiters adds to your bill. Trust your caterer's advice and don't skimp in this area, as it will affect your guests' comfort and the caterer's ability to keep things running smoothly. "Cater waiters" often do more than serve food. They may act as a setup crew to arrange your tables, place cards, centerpieces, and favors, and as presentation stylists, bartenders, kitchen help, restroom attendants, and cleanup crew.

d'oeuvre reception, or that ice sculpture you saw in a magazine? Even if they can't provide exactly what you have in mind, they should be able to suggest alternatives that will fit your vision and your budget. In this first conversation, request a rough idea of fees and sample menus. Will you have to provide the wedding cake, or is that included? Do they have a liquor license, or will you have to stock the bar? Will they serve the liquor if you provide it, and are there extra charges involved? What about other beverages, such as mixers, soft drinks, water, coffee, and tea? Can they supply any rentals

THE FOUR SEASONS

## Designer Drinks

| Summer | Autumn | Winter | Spring |
|---|---|---|---|
| Long Island iced tea | cranberry martini | hot toddy | vodka lemonade |
| mint julep | black velvet | brandy Alexander | bellini |
| mango margarita | mulled apple cider | eggnog | planter's punch |
| white sangria | Irish coffee | mulled wine | kiwi colada |
| sea breeze | toasted almond | flaming hot buttered rum | Georgia peach |

you'll require, or are they willing to coordinate arrangements with a rental company on your behalf? Inquire about their license and liability insurance. Find someone you click with—someone who understands your vision and has a "can-do" attitude. If your first impression on the phone is a good one, schedule a personal visit.

It is standard practice for caterers to ply you with tasty treats in order to give you an idea of what they are capable of and so that they can learn what you like. Many will give you an initial taste test on the first meeting and follow up with a more formal tasting as you begin

to determine the menu. Incorporating seasonal fare into your meal is often a delight for chefs because it gives them the opportunity to work with the choicest ingredients. Ask for suggestions and watch their imaginations soar: creamy white asparagus soup with pistachio puree, roasted lamb roulade with stuffed baby artichokes, wild mushroom risotto, or a full-scale clambake. Feel free to ask the caterer to prepare a new gourmet dish or a special family recipe, but remember that the greatest recipe for success is to select dishes that the caterer is familiar and comfortable with.

Plan to see the caterer in action at another wedding or similar event. This gives you the opportunity to judge food presentation under the appropriate conditions, as well as observe how well the staff functions with the guests. Remember, however, that you are being invited to someone else's affair and should act appropriately. Arrive properly dressed and on time, be unobtrusive, conduct your business, and depart before you wear out your welcome.

OPPOSITE: *Golden chopsticks prop up each place card and serve as a favor which will later remind your guests of the lovely eight-course banquet served at your reception.*

ABOVE: *Chocolate truffles are dressed with accents of pink and green, tying the edibles to the wedding's color palette. Served on butlered trays, the chocolates won't be given the chance to melt before making their way to guests.*

## A Helping Hand

Now that you're starting to get an idea of just how much is involved in planning a wedding, you may be wondering how you're going to find the time to manage it all. A professional wedding consultant can help you get and stay organized, steer you in the direction of reliable vendors, schedule meetings, make the most of your wedding budget, and even mediate disputes (with vendors or your future mother-in-law). A consultant can aid you in finding suitable locations, choosing and wording invitations, setting up appointments for dress fittings, and working with you to select table decor, menus, and floral arrangements. Whether you desire a professional's expertise and experience or you simply don't have the time to wade

through the research and labor of organizing a wedding, hiring someone to help with any or all of your plans is a benefit that should not be underestimated.

The wedding planner can be hired at any point in time to handle whatever portion of the arrangements you wish to delegate. This professional has seen it all and can help weed through the mountains of decisions you will have to make. If you are the hands-on type and enjoy the legwork, hire someone to help only on the wedding day itself. With someone in place to look after every detail and make sure your wishes are carried out, you are then free to be swept away by the celebration, rather than worrying if your place cards are properly alphabetized or if the caterer remembered to prepare a vegetarian meal for the best man. The consultant is your point person who will coordinate the vendors,

BELOW: *Pewter napkin rings are stacked and ready for action. Members of the catering staff will assemble all the elements for dressing the tables.*

maintain and adjust the schedule for the day, and troubleshoot in case questions or stumbling blocks arise.

If working on the entire event, the consultant's fee is usually a portion of the total budget, perhaps 10 to 15 percent. If hired only for the wedding day, an hourly fee or flat day rate applies.

If it's not possible (or desirable) to hire a professional, seek out an amiable friend or family member to act as coordinator at the event. Control freak or not, you will not enjoy being interrupted to solve problems on your wedding day. Delegate responsibility to someone else, go over all the details of your plans with them in advance, and make sure that all the vendors know who to approach on the wedding day with their inquiries.

ABOVE: *This modern space utilizes a dramatic cityscape as background scenery. The aisle-runner is lined on either side with petals to give the edges a finished look and lead the eye forward toward the altar.*

# Thank-You Etiquette

Each engagement, shower, or wedding gift you receive must be promptly recognized with a personalized note of thanks. Prior to the wedding, notes should be sent within two weeks of receipt of the present. For gifts received at or shortly after the wedding, a note should ideally be sent within one month. Some etiquette experts grant a grace period of up to three months, for gifts received at or immediately after the wedding, with the cautionary note that this extra time should be used only if absolutely necessary. Your notes can be short but must be handwritten and personal. Mention the gift specifically and offer your appreciation, either for the gift itself or the thought that went into choosing it. For a gift of money, try to indicate how you intend to use it.

## The Paper Chase

Your invitation is the first impression your guests have of your wedding, be it formal, semiformal, informal, or casual. It should relay the style of the event and who, what, when, and where, as well as how to respond. Whether you choose a stationer or decide to do it yourself, there are as many choices out there as you can envision. Pick and choose the items you want from the following list.

**"Save the date" cards:** Once your date is confirmed, these are sent out approximately six months prior to the wedding to alert guests of your plans. Use a formal announcement, a funky postcard, or even a handwritten note.

**Wedding invitation:** This may include inner and outer envelopes, a separate reception card, a pew card, a response card with a stamped envelope, and various informational inserts such as maps, directions, and hotel information.

**Program:** This outline of your wedding ceremony can include information about your wedding party, the order of the service, musical selections, poetry or readings, and any personal notes you wish to add, such as an explanation of a ritual or a word of thanks to your parents.

**Place cards:** Also called escort cards or tent cards, these inform guests of their seating assignments at the reception by including the guest's name and the appointed table number. A large seating chart is an interesting alternative to individual place cards.

**Table numbers:** A means of identifying each table, the numbers should enhance your tables' decor, not detract from it.

**Wedding announcements:** Sent after the wedding, and only to people who were not invited to the wedding, these follow wording similar to the invitation.

**Stationery or note cards:** These are used for thank-you notes for engagement, shower, and wedding gifts. If you're planning to monogram your stationery, remember that it is appropriate to use the initials of your groom's last name only after the wedding. Prior to that, use your maiden-name monogram for this stationery.

**At-home cards:** These are sent out after the wedding to inform people where you are now living.

ABOVE: *The wedding program shares the agenda of your marriage ceremony with your guests. In addition to the text, this creative couple used a photograph of themselves on layers of translucent vellum, attached to eye-catching handmade paper with gold-wired ribbon.*

Adding seasonal motifs to your invitations and wedding stationery is a fabulous way to make a unique statement. Choose beautiful papers, add graphics, emboss or deboss designs, or add color or gilding to spice up your paper goods. Petal papers are always a beautiful touch, and some are available with dormant seeds embedded in the paper so that your invitation literally can be planted and will sprout flowers. Add a snowflake, seashell, or leaf pattern, either by using a traditional printing process or by doing it yourself with a rubber stamp and embossing powder. If you have already chosen a color scheme, incorporate it into the invitations. Pressed flowers, seals and sealing wax, and die-cut shapes or elegant hole-punches can all be used to add zing to your invitations.

# Wedding Calligraphy

Calligraphy literally means "beautiful writing," and incorporating it into any part of your wedding stationery will add beauty and grace. Although it is very expensive to have each invitation or program lettered by hand, a professional calligrapher can create a master document that can then be printed via a commercial method. Calligraphers can be hired to address your envelopes, letter your place cards or favor tags, and create keepsakes such as a guest register or framed wedding certificate.

These days, many brides are looking for creative innovations, yet just as many are attracted to the traditional classics. The beauty of a simple printed invitation on fine paper will always be elegant and popular and will never go out of style. There are several common printing methods for wedding stationery.

**Engraving:** Elegant and expensive, this is the most formal printing method. The text is engraved into the paper, creating a raised impression that can be felt on either side of the paper. Keep in mind thicker paper stock allows for deeper engraving.

**Letterpress:** Another relief process, the letters are debossed into the paper rather than raised from it. This method has experienced a revival in popularity and is also very expensive.

**Thermography:** Resin is fused to the ink before it dries and made permanent with a heating process. The result is raised lettering that imitates engraving at a much lower cost.

**Offset lithography:** Ink is printed flat on the page and has a permanent matte finish.

**Laser or inkjet printing:** An option for many do-it-yourselfers, your computer's printer produces an image similar to lithography. Some home printers can produce artwork that is virtually indistinguishable from a traditional photograph to an untrained eye. Test the paper and ink together for bleeding and permanence.

## Band of Gold

Worn proudly for all the world to see, your rings are the symbols of your commitment to each other. Whether you each select a different design that reflects your individuality or decide on his-and-her matching wedding bands, you'll find this to be one of the most personal choices you'll make. Choosing a ring that has a seasonal touch may be as simple as a carved floral or leaf design, a heart-shaped stone or a ruby given on Valentine's Day, or a seasonal phrase engraved on the inside of your bands. But both engagement rings and wedding bands are truly seasonless, for any ring is appropriate year-round.

Your fiancé may have already chosen an engagement ring for you, or perhaps you will be inheriting a family heirloom. If you will be shopping for an engagement ring together, however, consider looking for your wedding bands at the same time. You'll have to decide if you'll want to wear both rings on one finger and if you want them to match or coordinate. Although classic styles can often be ordered quickly, a handcrafted ring can take as long as three to four months to be custom-made, and engraving an inscription inside the band can take up to a month during a jeweler's busiest seasons (think holidays and June weddings). Many gemstones are in style for both engagement and wedding bands, or an unbroken band of gold may be more to your liking. Choose a ring that is comfortable and appropriate to your lifestyle.

**Diamonds:** Perennially popular, the brilliant sparkle of a diamond is the number-one choice for wedding jewelry. Diamonds are graded on carat, clarity, cut, and color, traits known in the trade as the "four Cs."

**Precious gems:** Stones such as sapphires, emeralds, and rubies are once again popular for both engagement rings and wedding bands.

**Semiprecious stones:** A wealth of fabulous gemstones can be included in your rings, such as garnets, pearls, lapis, and malachite.

**Platinum:** The strongest and most costly metal commonly used in jewelry, it has a gray-white color similar to silver.

**Gold:** Naturally yellow in color, gold is generally mixed with other alloys to add strength to the soft metal. Twenty-four-karat gold is pure, with no alloys, but not practical for daily wear. Choose a ring of eighteen- or fourteen-karat gold.

**Colored gold:** Different metal alloys are mixed with pure yellow gold to change its hue. Some of the common choices are white, pink, and green gold.

**Sterling silver:** Though a less common choice than gold or platinum, the luminescent beauty and lasting quality of sterling silver should not be discounted, particularly if cost is an issue.

OPPOSITE: *An emerald-cut diamond engagement ring set in platinum along with the calligraphy on the invitation show off the contemporary yet classic style of this couple's wedding.*

ABOVE: *Many women opt for a wedding band set with precious stones. This assortment of handcrafted engagement and wedding rings shows that there are stunning choices for someone looking for a truly unique piece of jewelry.*

## Chapter Three

# Summer

*J*ust say the word "summer" and you can feel the golden rays of sunshine beaming down from a dazzling blue sky and enveloping you in a rush of warmth. An occasional puff of wispy white cloud floats by in a shape that reminds you of a sailboat, and you can't wait to take your shoes off and run through the green grass. You love the sensation of the season. Tranquil, unhurried, and a little unstructured…yet with an unstoppable supply of energy—these two seemingly contradictory states blend flawlessly.

The summer wedding takes all this in and translates it for the occasion. An informal event reigns supreme at this time of year, and even a black-tie affair will benefit from a dose of summer's frame of mind. A touch of whimsy, a splash of color, a shady pair of Adirondack chairs for a private moment with your new hubby—let your celebration shine with the freedom of summer.

Presented here is a gallery of ideas for your summer wedding. Think of this section, and its three counterparts, as snapshots of seasonal style. Several concepts are described in the text, with many more hands-on examples of the big picture shown in photographs. Choose just a few charming details, or drape your event in the mood of the month—just make sure your wedding is "well seasoned."

## The Summer Barbecue

After a midmorning ceremony, wedding party and guests stroll en masse to a nearby park, where brightly striped tents provide a shady retreat from the noonday sun. The grandeur of the event is not lost in the easygoing spirit of this time of year. All dressed up for the wedding, the tent is a festive haven, with flaps raised to enjoy the full effect of the glorious day. The abundant baskets of blue hydrangeas, morning glories, and perfect white peonies that decorate the ceremony have been given a second life, magically transported to the reception ahead of the guests. Baskets hang around the perimeter of the tent frame, their trails of ivy and deep purple petunias forming a lacy curtain. Far

ABOVE: *Make use of every available space and keep guests circulating. Here, a shaded porch is a quiet spot for guests to refill their glasses and enjoy a view of the harbor.*

OPPOSITE: *Travel in style! The wedding party and guests are ferried over to their reception location under the watchful eye of a famous landmark.*

below the tented top, a blue and white tiled ballroom floor echoes the colors of the day in endless repetition. Even the tent poles are decked out for the event, wrapped from head to toe in gossamer netting and climbing clematis winding its way upward from floor baskets toward the pale blue and white striped roof.

Guests are greeted as they arrive and directed to their table assignments by the newlyweds' ushers, who are performing their final duties of the day. Long tables rest end to end for the entire length of the tent and are covered in crisp white linen. Each guest finds a pair of blue and white hem-stitched napkins waiting, which are banded together with a rustic pewter napkin ring. Guests will need the extra wiping power: this is a barbecue, after all. The centerpieces repeat the theme of summery baskets; clusters of them in varying small sizes burst with the colors of blue, white, and purple flowers. They create a staccato row trailing down the central line of the long tables, intermingled with glowing candles that add romance. At the end of the day, every guest will be invited to take home one of these little basket centerpieces.

The catering staff, dressed in white short-sleeved shirts, khaki shorts, and powder blue bow ties, is already circulating through the crowd with trays filled with skewered bites and other mouthwatering treats. On this pass, you choose a skewer of garlicky swordfish, dipped delicately in peppered mango salsa, and enjoy it while wandering over to tap your foot to the music of the bluegrass band. Belly up to the bar, where the keg is primed and the beer is ice-cold. Or help yourself to a glass of pink lemonade or pink champagne, served with a ruby red strawberry balanced on the edge of the glass. A fleet of grills is lined up like soldiers standing ready; the chef gives orders to his team as the coals blaze red-hot. Just about everything tastes better when it's

ABOVE: *This perky cake with fondant frosting can really take the heat! Fondant is a wonderful choice for an outdoor wedding. It can be on display for hours without melting or spoiling.*

grilled…soon the smells of dinner roasting will start your stomach growling. Each place setting has a gift to the guest: a bottle of the father of the groom's secret hot-sauce recipe, beautifully wrapped in handmade paper that's the perfect shade of blue. A vellum strip with the wedding date inscribed on it holds everything in place. If summer means informal, this is heaven.

## The Seaside Wedding

Guests check their shoes at the boardwalk and follow a path outlined in shells, cattails, and tall torches to an area closer to the shore. A few beach chairs are provided for those who might need them and are decorated gaily with small clusters of flowers and sea grasses. Several people have come prepared with beach blankets. Most stand about and chat while they wait, though a few adventurous sorts steal down to the water's edge and dip their toes in the ocean to test the temperature. The groom, looking dapper in his white dinner jacket, digs his bare feet into the warm sand untill he reaches a cool spot below. As the sun heads toward the horizon, the torches light the way for the procession of bridesmaids. Mermaids would be more accurate—their iridescent chiffon gowns shimmer with the colors of the sea and gently flare below the knee, foreshadowing the coming of the bride. She arrives at last, a vision in her creamy white chiffon mermaid gown. Her sweep train trails behind her in the sand like the mermaid's tail. Toenails

ABOVE: *Salads take all forms for a summer buffet. The freshest ingredients add brilliant color to the catch of the day, grilled to perfection.*

peek from under the flared bottom of her dress as she walks, revealing shimmery blue polish the exact shade of the bridesmaids' dresses. A short veil does not mask the strapless top of this sexy gown, as soft wisps of tulle float in the breeze, firmly attached to a crystal tiara. Her bouquet reverberates with brilliant color—blue and purple and coral and pale, pale green. Four tall bamboo poles—each topped with a burst of the same flowers in different assortments—are anchored deep into the sand to define the four corners of the altar. Bride and groom step into the space together and speak their vows above the sound of waves as the setting sun sends out a brilliant show of red and orange and purple.

Cocktails are served on a deck overlooking the beach. Upon arrival, guests find their seating assignments nestled in a tabletop bed of sand, each name carefully inscribed on one side of a sand dollar, the table number on the other side, and all perfectly alphabetized. The moon is full tonight, illuminating the black waves breaking against the shore, but flaming torches and galvanized lanterns add dramatic lighting to the scene. There are many tasty hors d'oeuvres to choose from, and seafood prevails, of course. A raw bar is kept cool on a block of crystal-clear ice sculpted into the form of a giant open clamshell. Waiters pass trays of delectable hors d'oeuvres— some presented on a colorful bed of smooth sea glass, others on a tangle of black seaweed, and still others on a mound of glittering sea salt. A special cocktail has been chosen for tonight's event—a sea breeze, of course—and just as you're thinking about getting another, the doors are opened to the main reception room.

Inside, the walls are aglow with twinkling fairy lights wrapped in metallic sheers, causing each tiny light to burst into a star. On the tables, frosted glass plates look like pieces of

BELOW: *This napkin is touched by the sea at this beach wedding. A sand dollar attached to a ribbon printed with the couple's names and the wedding date stands in for a napkin ring.*

polished beach glass perched atop cobalt chargers, a fitting contrast to sparkling crystal stemware. A parade of tuxedoed waiters sweeps in with the first course—crispy crab napoleons—and you're hoping that the groom's favorite food will be following…lobster. The newlyweds take their first turn around the dance floor to the Beach Boys' "Wouldn't It Be Nice?" This is a dancing crowd, and the orchestra keeps everyone on their feet between each course. It's a good thing, too, because the wedding cake looks exquisite, decorated with chocolate shells and golden sugar coral, and you want to work off some of your meal before the cake is cut. When it's time to depart, the newlyweds, spending their first night as husband and wife on a neighboring island, make their exit via speedboat. This is black tie summer style, and no conventional rules need apply.

ABOVE: *Natural light has a warm beauty that envelops a summer bride wearing a strapless, sequined, and embroidered bodice with box pleat skirt.*

OPPOSITE: *This couple found a dramatic photo opportunity where sea meets sand. Whenever possible, use the elements of your location to highlight the seasonal aspects of your event.*

ABOVE: *Candles are nestled in sand and protected against the wind by containers of varying shapes and sizes. A smattering of shells intermingles with wildflowers in this interesting centerpiece grouping created for a beach wedding.*

# Secrets of Summer

➤ Ask your florist to make flower-covered parasols for your bridesmaids.

➤ Outfit your attendants in lacy cotton sundresses and white straw sun hats festooned with flowers to match their bouquets.

➤ Decorate sugar cookies in fanciful shapes, such as ladybugs, butterflies, and dragonflies, and wrap them in petal paper for favors.

➤ Build your entire centerpiece of fresh green and flowering herbs arranged in clay pots or galvanized tubs.

➤ For your big send-off, fill petal cones with flower and grass seeds, and let the wind sprinkle them somewhere they can grow.

➤ Hang glass canning jars from tree branches with flowing ribbons, then light up the night with votive candles inside some while floating flowers in others.

➤ Use a wheelbarrow as a tub for keeping beverages cold.

➤ As a tongue-in-cheek nod to our pesky little friends, have a parade of chocolate ants climb in formation to the top tier of your strawberry shortcake wedding cake.

➤ Put your flower girl in fairy wings for a midsummer night's dream.

➤ Provide fans to guests—as programs, favors, and seating cards.

➤ Cut the stems of large blooms, such as hydrangeas or peonies, short enough to fit into a water tube. Then insert the tubes into the ground or sand so that only the blossoms remain visible. This is a great way to create an aisle or altar outdoors.

➤ Build your entire bar out of crystal-clear ice—the type used for ice sculptures. Create smaller decorative containers with fruit and flowers frozen in the water to keep vodka and champagne on ice.

➤ Wildflowers gathered into a loose, hand-tied bouquet are just right for summer.

➤ Hurricane vases are great for outdoor weddings; they provide wind protection to keep candles glowing brightly. Dress yours up with flowers or shells surrounding the bottom of a pillar candle.

➤ Instead of a unity candle, the bride and groom can pour sand into a single canister to represent the blending of their lives into an inseparable larger entity.

## Chapter Four

# A Stylish Marriage

ABOVE: *Clusters of pillar candles sit amidst a scattering of rose petals. Remember to keep candles away from the active areas on a table to prevent guests from accidental contact with the flames.*

OPPOSITE: *The tight, round shape of this charming nosegay, constructed primarily of roses, gets variety from the different hues of the flowers.*

With your critical decisions of when and where made, you're free to start thinking about what and how: what will your wedding look like, and how will you tie the key components together to create a style that is unique and personal? The trimmings and trappings of a wedding must fit their surroundings, particularly when you're styling the celebration to reflect the time of year. When selecting colors, flowers, and table settings to adorn your ceremony and reception, be aware of the environment. When it's all put together, the impression will be memorable.

One of the essential elements you can use to do this is color. Color is emotional at a fundamental level; it creates moods, evokes feelings. We gravitate toward certain colors in our daily lives, judiciously dressing our homes and ourselves, laying down a foundation, handpicking and coordinating each accessory and embellishment. Your wedding should be dressed with the same careful attention to detail, and choosing a color palette is a great way to organize the look. Using a common palette throughout the wedding will unify its various facets, helping each visually flow into the next. Attire, flowers for ceremony and reception, table linens, your cake, stationery items, and favors can all reflect your color scheme.

The color palette is one of the elements you'll consider when selecting the flowers for your wedding. Shape, scent, variety, and even sentiment will also come into play as you choose bouquets and boutonnieres, centerpieces, and floral accents. The floral arrangements you select will speak of your individuality and be one of the primary marks of style in your event. Your choices today are unlimited, and there is no better way to impart a seasonal approach than through your wedding flowers.

Attention to detail is most evident when it comes to table decor. The reception tables are where your guests will spend the majority of the wedding, up close and personal. Take care in crafting the table settings as well as the surrounding areas. The most obvious points to attend to are making sure your guests are comfortable and have everything they need at their fingertips. Beyond that, surround

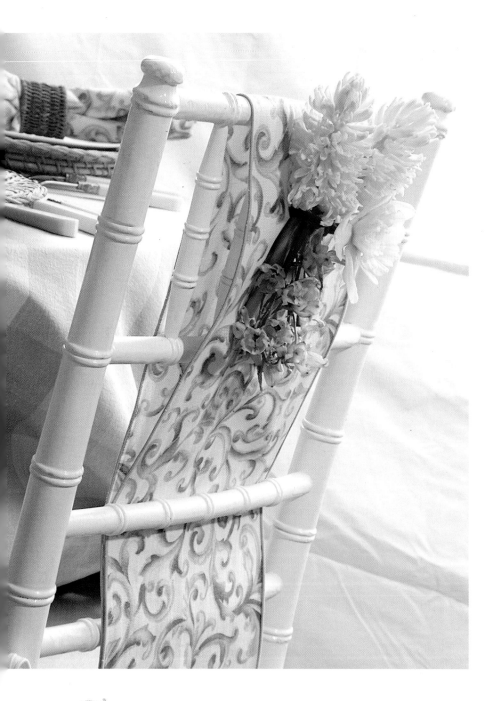

them in style; give them beautiful things to look at. Linens, tableware, centerpieces, and other table accents can all help make the wedding beautiful and harmonious with the season.

## Dreaming in Color

Developing a palette is one of the major style decisions everyone thinks about when it comes to wedding planning. Color can tie the elements of the wedding together into a cohesive whole, even if no other theme or overall style is chosen. Use the ceremony and reception locations as starting points, and select accents that will enhance their characteristics rather than fight for attention. Often color is selected for attire and flowers and then carried through to the table settings and other accents. Use varying tints in one color family, similar tones of complementary colors, or colors that border each other on the color wheel to add depth to your designs. If the decor of the two sites is extremely different, add neutral colors to tie them together. Use muted tones for your bouquets and centerpieces that pick up highlights from both locations, dress your bridesmaids in mushroom or pewter, and use a similar neutral color for the table linens, or simply opt for white or cream. Although there is a lovely harmony in using one palette for the entire event, it is not always necessary to coordinate every single hue chosen

ABOVE: *Fabric can be tied into a bow or woven through the backs of chairs to add visual interest to the room. Here, the chair ties match the napkins, and are secured to the back of the guests' chairs with a sprig of hyacinth and delphinium.*

for the wedding. If you have your heart set on your attendants wearing a color that would look dreadful on the tables in the reception room, by all means mix it up. Don't worry about the maids clashing with the room. After all, you can't dress everyone that will be at the wedding! When was the last time you noticed that someone's outfit didn't match their surroundings? If anything, be mindful of the ceremony area, as well as the location where formal portraits will be taken, when selecting colors for attendants and bouquets.

Places to add color to the wedding:

- invitations
- programs
- wedding-party attire
- wedding-party flowers and ribbons
- floral accents at the ceremony
- huppah or wedding canopy
- your rings or other jewelry
- place cards
- table linens
- chair covers
- centerpieces and candles
- decoration at the reception
- lighting
- favors
- food, including the wedding cake
- special reception cocktail or punch
- guest book

There are many approaches to choosing wedding colors. Find inspiration in a favorite flower or fabric. Take your cue from the ceremony or reception site. Consider the complexions of your bridesmaids when selecting dress colors, or put the attendants in a neutral color and use accents such as gloves, wraps, and flowers to bring in stronger colors. Incorporate a piece of your family history into the wedding and build your colors around that, such as a treasured quilt to adorn the cake table or an embroidered ring pillow that has been used in every family wedding for four generations. Or, walk over to your local hardware store to look at paint swatches and try different combinations until you find something that speaks to you (or until the sales clerk asks you to leave!).

ABOVE: *Use the colors of your reception site to best advantage. The palette of blues and purples is picked up in the table's painted overcloth, the stemware, the embroidered napkins, the candleholders, and the flowers. Rented sheer chair covers and floral nosegays add a bit of veiled romance to white ballroom chairs.*

# Color Your World

| Summer | Autumn |
|---|---|
| azure | cranberry |
| goldenrod | mustard |
| fern | brick red |
| rose | moss green |
| pearl | navy |
| tangerine | plum |
| lime | amber |
| turquoise | copper |
| wisteria | mocha |

| Winter | Spring |
|---|---|
| claret | cottage blue |
| eggplant | terra-cotta |
| Wedgwood | berry |
| spruce | banana |
| ruby | shell pink |
| cinnamon | cantaloupe |
| gold | mint |
| lapis | aqua |
| platinum | lilac |

Of course, certain seasons automatically evoke color associations: bright colors in summer; deep reds, oranges, and browns in autumn; jewel tones in winter; and pastels in spring. These natural fits instantly infuse the event with seasonal style. Yet most colors can be made to work at any time of year, so don't feel you have to limit your options if you want to choose something less archetypal. Here are some examples.

**White:** Thanks to its traditional connotations, an all-white wedding can be breathtaking year-round. Work with textures to tie it to the season: chiffon in summer or damask in winter, different shades of white flowers in your bouquet, and lights everywhere you look.

**White plus one:** Add one color to an otherwise white wedding to emphasize focal points.

**Neutrals:** Colors such as ivory, champagne, taupe, sable, navy, steel, or black are an easy fit for tricky situations and add elegance to their surroundings.

**Muted or pastel colors:** Muted shades have black added to the pure color—burgundy instead of red, for example. Pastel tints have white added to the pure color. Think outside the box: ice blue in winter, garnet in fall, apricot in summer, thistle in spring.

**Soft colors:** Tones that have both black and white in them—sage, heather, copen blue—have a sense of quiet about them.

**Dramatic colors:** Intensity and contrast create a stunning statement. Brilliant colors such as fuchsia, chartreuse, and cobalt blue are attention-grabbers. Add black to your color scheme (think pink and black, black and white, or black and honeysuckle) for extra pizzazz.

**Metallics:** Gold, silver, platinum, brass, bronze, and copper add sparkle and luster whether used as accents or as a main color theme. Incorporate metals or metallic fabrics, such as an iridescent sheer or a silk lamé.

There are a few principles to remember. Bright, intense color protrudes and vibrates, making objects seems larger. Dull or dark color recedes and minimizes. Using complementary colors of pure intensity together will create an explosion for your eyes. The colors will pulse and pop. Soften the effect by using tints or shades of the colors. Colors that sit next to each other on the color wheel form a pleasant partnership, as will a selection of tints and shades of one hue. Here are some terms to familiarize yourself with.

**primary colors:** red, yellow, and blue

**secondary colors:** orange, green, and purple

**complementary colors:** sit opposite each other on the color wheel

**analogous colors:** sit next to each other on the color wheel

**hue:** the name of a color in its pure form (that is, yellow or green)

**intensity:** brightness or purity of the color

**tint:** color with white added to it

**shade:** color with black added to it

## Budding Romance

The aisle is trimmed with them, the altar defined by them. You clutch a big blowsy bunch as you walk on a carpet of them.

ABOVE: *Grape hyacinth is wrapped in satin ribbon secured with pearl-tipped pins. Fragrant white gardenias will be secured in the bridesmaids' hairdos with bobby pins.*

They provide a warm welcome for your guests' first impression and a cheery center to the evening's repast. Flowers are everywhere you turn at a wedding, joyously announcing the importance of the day. Breathe in, and their heady perfume intoxicates you; glance around at their glorious vivacity. Flowers are forever linked with romance and special occasions, and their pleasures can be overwhelming.

Some floral designers may book up to a year in advance, so don't delay in getting your search started. When choosing a floral designer for your wedding, be prepared for your first meeting. You'll have to discuss the ceremony and reception locations; bring pictures if you have them. The florist will want to know about your dress and the wedding party's attire (again, bring pictures if available; fabric swatches are also helpful) as well as the size and level of formality of the event. Look in magazines, catalogs, and books to get an idea of the flower types, shapes, and sizes you find pleasing for bouquets and centerpieces, and bring the references with you. Some designers can copy a photograph

Opposite: *Floral features add a dramatic effect to an outdoor event. A bountiful bouquet accents the ends of alternating aisle chairs, while a carpet of fresh petals awaits the arrival of the bridal party. A garland at the entrance to the central aisle alerts guests to seat themselves from the outside in, leaving the floral carpet in pristine condition for the processional.*

to the letter, but you may get more bang for your buck by remaining open-minded to the florist's suggestions. Look at samples of the designer's work: see if you like the style and if you think the designer understands what you are looking for. And be honest about the limits of your budget. You may have an approach in mind that requires expensive, exotic, or out-of-season flowers, but a good designer will make suggestions for fitting alternatives that will still give you the overall effect you fell in love with—without breaking the bank.

Selecting seasonal blossoms adds appropriate style besides being cost-effective. Flower availability can vary greatly from region to region and sometimes even florist to florist. Check with your designer as to what will be in season at the time of your wedding, as well as other economical, year-round flower choices. Your flower budget is often 10 percent of your total wedding cost and can easily grow to many thousands of dollars if unrestrained, so if you have a ceiling to your spending, make sure your designer knows that the sky is not the limit. While you are deciding on the arrangements, remember this rule of thumb: the less labor-intensive, the better the price. A gifted designer can craft a stunning floral display for you at any budget. In fact, many have indicated that their dream client is one who has an overall impression of the style and color she wants (such as "spring, informal, using blues and purples") and the type and number of pieces required (for example, the number of bouquets, boutonnieres, and centerpieces), then gives the florist full artistic license to create any way he wishes. This gives the designer the opportunity to take full advantage of the freshest, most beautiful, most reasonable blossoms at the market in the days before your wedding.

Often a bride will use her bouquet as a starting point, choosing flowers for herself first, then unifying her attendants' bouquets with similar flowers and adding boutonnieres for her groom and his ushers. The next step is building those flowers into centerpieces, adding and subtracting, altering the blossoms slightly so that each item has its own distinctive flavor yet fits with every other. Can you summarize your concept in a few general impressions: spring garden, orchid cascade, handpicked formal roses? Any of these impressions can inspire an entire theme to weave throughout your wedding. A single

flower—such as a rose, daisy, or lily—can be the inspiration for a themed floral treatment, as well as an underlying current for styling the rest of the wedding, using that one bloom throughout the details of the wedding.

With your florist's help, assess the environment. Visit the sites together if possible, and narrow down a plan. If you are to be married outdoors in a beautiful garden, you may not need any floral accents for your ceremony. If your wedding is in a stunning location, be it simple or ornate, you want to enhance its beauty, not detract by over-dressing it. Avoid overpowering scents that might interfere with the taste and aroma of food, clash with your perfume, or bring on an allergy attack in your minister.

After your initial meetings, the designer will provide you with a full proposal, out-lining the numbers of bouquets and centerpieces, the types of flowers to be used, setup and delivery time, cost, deposits, and payment schedule. Be prepared to put down a deposit as soon as you are ready to go to contract to reserve the date. However, if you make this commitment far in advance, you may not begin the final confirmation of your designs until much closer to the wedding (perhaps two or three months in advance).

When your wedding day arrives, your flowers should be delivered well misted and wrapped in cellophane for protection. Keep them away from heat or direct sun. If received the night before the event, keep them in a dark, cool place, and provide a water source only as instructed by the florist. Beware of the refrigerator, as a home refrigerator is a very dry environment for flowers—placing them inside with certain foods or fruit will ruin them.

When choosing the style of your bouquet, keep body size and shape in mind as well as attire. The bouquet should not overpower the person, nor should it be so small that its effect is lost. A larger or taller woman can handle a bigger bouquet than someone of petite size. Also, consider how the flowers and style of your bouquet coordinate with your gown. A grand dress should pair up with an impressive bouquet, but the embellishments of both should balance each other. A simpler dress provides a frame for a more elaborate bouquet, whereas the same flowers would compete with a gown with ornate beading or lace. Your flowers should not be heavy or cumbersome, but rather easy to hold and well proportioned.

ABOVE: *Many floral designers carefully cradle bouquets in tissue to prevent them from being crushed in transit. A covering of cellophane keeps them from drying out.*

**Constructed bouquet:** Clusters of flowers are taped or wired together to create a structured form. The stems might be completely enclosed with ribbon, or the wired stems can be inserted into a bouquet holder.

**Nosegay:** A tight, round bouquet. A very small nosegay is a posy. A nosegay made of concentric rings, each ring created from a different flower or color, is called a Beidermeier.

**Hand-tied:** Flowers have a "just picked" effect, as if you went into the garden and

grabbed a handful. Stems are tied (sometimes taped first) with a bow at a central place to anchor them, and some of the stems are left exposed.

**Cascade**: Flowers and greenery trail downward from the main body of the bouquet.

**Pomander**: A small to medium-size sphere is covered with flowers and suspended from a ribbon handle.

**Composite**: One large, dramatic blossom is created by wiring individual petals or flowers together to look like a single enormous flower.

**Breakaway**: Two or more bouquets are nestled together to create a larger bouquet for the ceremony. Possibilities include a section that is removed and becomes the groom's boutonniere, which the bride pins on his lapel when she reaches him at the altar, or one spray for keeping and one for throwing. A charming new alternative arranges many miniature bouquets together to give the illusion of one composition. When the bride tosses her bouquet to her eager single friends, it breaks apart into multiple lucky posies.

When planning the flowers for your wedding, here are the items to consider.

**Bridal bouquet:** White is elegant and traditional, and can have added depth when different hues of white and cream flowers are mixed together. A colored bouquet, sometimes the bride's only opportunity to harmonize with the color scheme, will show up beautifully in photographs.

**Attendants' flowers:** Choose blooms that complement your bouquet on a smaller scale.

**Boutonnieres:** Worn in the left jacket lapel by the groom, groomsmen, fathers, and grandfathers, these blooms will have no water source for the entire day, so they need to be hardy. Echo the flowers used in the bouquets, and set the groom apart with a special touch to his boutonniere, such as an added sprig of rosemary or a unique flower.

**Other personal flowers**: These include corsages for mothers, grandmothers, and honored guests; baskets, wreaths, or nosegays for flower girls; flowers for your hair or headpiece; and flowers to adorn your dress, purse, or even shoes.

**Flowers for the ceremony**: You'll need arrangements to adorn the altar and stairs, to decorate the aisle chairs, or to highlight the basket holding the ceremony programs. Add props swathed in flowers to define the space—a birdbath or a wheelbarrow, a huppah or an arch, floral pedestals to create a portal, or a welcoming wreath—and, of course, petals to be scattered in the aisle prior to the bride's grand entrance.

**Centerpieces**: Create a focal point for each table. Centerpieces should be either lower or higher than eye level so as not to interfere with guests' line of sight or cut off the pleasant flow of conversation. Use interesting containers for seasonal sway: baskets, mason jars, rustic urns, watering cans, or cornucopias. Vary your containers or even the colors of the flower arrangements from table to table.

ABOVE: *Honor special guests with floral treats. Have your designer create a personal expression of love for every member of the family.*

**Room decor**: Guests will feel welcomed when the first thing they see is a floral highlight setting the stage. Use a wreath, garland, or spray on the front door. Potted plants and trees can conceal unsightly areas or close up large unused spaces, or dress folding screens with flowers and greenery for the same purpose. Add floral accents to your napkin rings and menu, make sundry baskets for the rest rooms, and don't forget about arrangements for the gift and escort card tables. Ask the florist to move flowers after the ceremony and bring them to the reception, or ask your attendants to place their bouquets on these tables until the end of the event. Columns, a fireplace mantel, doorways, chandeliers, a stair banister, and even trees will benefit from some extra budding attention.

**Flowers and food:** Include unsprayed flowers in the decorations for your cake and set a divine table for it with a lush display. Catering trays for hors d'oeuvres and buffet tables need embellishment—you can even use edible flowers in the food itself.

You can get any flower you want (almost) anytime you want it, but out-of-season blossoms can be extremely pricey. Flower availability throughout the year is different in every area, and many flowers cross over from one season to the next or may be closely associated with a season but readily available in most months. Use the following list only as a means to get your ideas jump-started.

**All year:** rose, orchid, stephanotis, gardenia, lily

**Summer:** hydrangea, daisy, ranunculus, bougainvillea, gerbera daisy, sweet pea, delphinum, Queen Anne's lace, peony, astilbe, cosmos

**Autumn:** dahlia, sunflower, orange blossom, chrysanthemum, aster, waxflower, anemone, black-eyed Susan, bittersweet, 'Casablanca' lily, coxcomb

**Winter:** amaryllis, paperwhite, seeded eucalyptus, holly, mistletoe, violet, pepperberry, stock, poinsettia, snowberry, juniper

**Spring:** lily of the valley, hyacinth, forsythia, viburnum, iris, tulip, daffodil, magnolia, cherry blossom, freesia, lilac

ABOVE: *A bouquet does not have to be large to have impact. The saturated hues in this compact nosegay draw the eye to its spectacular presentation.*

OPPOSITE: *Calla lilies are dramatic in any color. Their sculptural contours are carefully held in place by a taut ribbon casing.*

## The Perfect Setting

After using color as your foundation and flowers as your focal points, you will further define your space with tableware, lighting and candles, and interesting decorative touches. The impact of the whole reception room will make an imprint on your guests the moment they see it, and each additional detail should be a delight to their senses.

Guests' tables should look full but not too busy. You don't want to distract your guests from the evening's festivities. Make sure each person has enough room to sit and eat without feeling cramped or claustrophobic, can get up without banging into someone or something, and does not have to confine his or her normal movements for fear of hitting a neighbor. A sixty-inch (96.5cm) round table can seat eight comfortably and ten snuggly, but more than that is a very tight fit. These tables are generally pretty unsightly

# Budding Suggestions

## Summer

Choose hearty blooms that can withstand heat and won't wilt easily. Keep personal flowers in water as long as possible, or make sure they will have a source, such as a small water tube, to keep them fresh all day. Avoid drips and stains on your dress by asking someone to dry the stems of your bouquet before you take it. Have each of your attendants carry a bouquet made of clusters of one type of flower in a single color scheme. For your bouquet, incorporate all of the varieties of flowers they are carrying.

## Autumn

Pressed, dried leaves, and other ornamental grasses can comprise very interesting and vibrant arrangements, and are also a great seasonal filler. Wire them in clusters of fiery color to incorporate into centerpieces and bouquets. Hydrangeas, which have been growing all summer long, are at their heartiest in early fall. Cover a basket completely with moss; wire in some gilded nuts, dried pods, and pinecones; and fill with dried lavender for the guests to toss in handfuls as the bride and groom exit the ceremony.

## Winter

Many churches, hotels, and public places such as museums don festive attire for the holidays. This adds up to big savings for you because you'll have far less decorating to do. Groups of potted poinsettias in red and white create a cheerful breakaway centerpiece that your guests can take home at the end of the wedding. Create a floral focal point on a fireplace mantel with a topiary made of evergreens and snowberries. Add accents of color by using pepperberries and holly berries.

## Spring

Potted flowering plants are abundant and reasonably priced. So be generous when decorating with flowers. Use a different variety on each table, or mix several together in a beautiful container for a miniature spring garden. Add fragrant edible blossoms to lemonade or punch for both color and delicate flavor. Line your aisle with trowels of Easter grass dotted sporadically with colorful tulips or delicate lily of the valley. In lieu of rice or birdseed for your exit, offer wildflower seeds to your guests.

and should be covered with tablecloths that extend to the floor and hide the table's unattractive legs. As with many other wedding details, white is the traditional color used for table linens, but these days, weddings can be dressed with brilliant color and unusual materials without losing their romantic ambience.

When choosing linens, many aspects such as color, fabric, pattern, and texture all come into play. Choose colors in your palette or select a neutral as a foundation for other details. Use different colors on different tables for an interesting and informal look. Tablecloths and napkins are available in solid colors or a multitude of patterns. Florals for every season add vivacity to the room. Paisleys, stripes, checks, polka dots, fleurs-de-lis, and other motifs will lend visual interest economically over a large surface area. Napkins can coordinate or contrast with the tablecloths. Some fabrics seem more

ABOVE: *Create the feel of a picnic by using a fine linen checked cloth and matching chair pads at your afternoon garden party. Here, even the garden sculptures have been dressed for the occasion.*

OPPOSITE: *An arrangement of pastel roses, green viburnum, and white lilacs adds elegance to the rented silver compote and lovely patterned tablecloth.*

appropriate at certain times of year—a heavy brocade or satin damask in fall or winter; a light chintz, cotton pique, or airy Swiss dot in spring or summer. Others are appropriate year-round—linen, dupioni silk, iridescent sheers, or lace. Beading, embroidery, and overlays all add layers of interest to the table dressings.

Your other table accoutrements should coordinate with and build on the choice of linens. Dishes can be simple or distinct, and the same is true of flatware. Fine china or

# Everything Under the Sun

Many reception halls have a fabulous assortment of table linens to choose from, while others may be able to provide only the basics. If you are working with a raw space or merely want to supplement the coffers of your reception hall, the place to look is a party rental company. While some rental companies may specialize in tents or linens only, others offer one-stop shopping when it comes to ordering whatever you might need. Fundamentals such as tents and flooring, heaters, air-conditioners, industrial-size grills, portable cooking and refrigeration equipment, and generators can be found through a rental company. Round and rectangular tables, wooden folding chairs and ballroom chairs in every color imaginable, an assortment of china and flatware, stemware, linens, silver trays, and serving pieces (as well as a host of other materials) are all available for your selection. Decorative items such as compote dishes or urns for centerpieces, candlesticks and candelabras, votives, chair covers and ties, and objects such as chandeliers, columns, statues, decorative arches, and benches can all be rented for the day.

Call to find out what is available from your local rental company, and make an appointment with a salesperson to visit the showroom. Samples of selections will be displayed so that you can see and touch everything. The salespeople are extremely knowledgeable. Let them know the style of the event, your likes and dislikes, your budget, and any ideas you have already finalized (such as color or flowers), and ask for their input. Set up a sample table to try your choices, and when you find something you like, take an instant or digital photo to show your florist or event designer. Rentals might be harder to come by during the holidays, when many other events are taking place, so don't wait until the last minute. Find out when a firm commitment is needed and what sorts of deposits are necessary, and get an itemized contract of everything you have ordered. Rentals may be delivered the day before or the day of the event and picked up anywhere from the night of the event to one or two days afterward. Coordinate this with the reception hall. Make sure your caterer has a copy of the rental list, so that he or she can check that all the items arrived as ordered and are accounted for and packed up for the rental company to pick up.

# Setting the Table

Your table may be preset with any or all of the following elements, depending on the type of food service you have planned.

**Charger:** An oversize plate that acts as a placeholder on the table to avoid an empty space when a plated dinner is being served. In the most formal service, the charger is removed when the meal is served.

**Dinner plate:** The large plate on which the main meal is served. For buffet service, dinner plates are usually stacked at the beginning of the buffet line.

**Salad plate:** A small plate or bowl that might be preset and individually filled at the table by the waiter or filled in the kitchen and placed in front of the seated guest.

**Soup bowl:** As with the salad plate, a soup bowl may be filled either in the kitchen or directly at the place setting.

**Bread plate:** A very small plate, often with an accompanying bread knife, that is placed above the dinner plate on the upper left.

**Flatware:** Utensils are arranged on either side of the plate in the order in which they'll be used. For example, a fish fork for an appetizer or a salad fork would be placed on the outside edge of the dinner fork. Forks are set on the left of the plate, knives (with sharp edge pointing toward the plate) and spoons on the right. Dessert forks and spoons are set above the plate perpendicular to the other utensils. Sometimes flatware is arranged decoratively on the plate or napkin.

**Stemware:** Glasses are placed above the dinner plate on the upper right. They, too, should be placed in the order in which they'll be used. Choices for typical stemware include champagne, white wine, red wine, and water glasses.

**Other items:** Salt and pepper shakers or cellars should be available on the table, as should dishes for butter. These items can be provided in miniature for each individual guest or in large size for family-style service.

rustic stoneware, patterned or colored, can be rented, as can multipatterned utensils in silver and gold tones or with handles made of other materials. Choose stemware based on the formality of the event. Handblown stemware will fit just about any style, while cut crystal should be reserved for the most formal affairs. Colored glass usually creates a less formal look.

Other table details and decorations are the jewels you'll use to finish the look. Silver place-card holders, glittering candles, fabric garlands, calligraphed table numbers, and printed menus give ornament and dimension to the surfaces. Add a small floral detail to each place setting—a colored eggshell or a hollowed miniature pumpkin forms a seasonal container to house a tea light or tiny floral arrangement. Napkins are a wonderful focal point for detail. Folded into lovely shapes and fastened with elegant rings, they add finish to the tabletop. Do something interesting to spice up your napkins. Use rings of wicker for summer, or bear grass or ivy in spring; hot-glue an assortment of miniature pinecones and gilded nuts to a coppery ribbon for autumn; put together a cluster of golden jingle bells for winter. Tuck seasonal flora into the folds of the napkin, affix flowers to the ring, or merely set an audacious bloom on top of it.

Lighting is an extremely important and often forgotten element when styling your celebration. Lighting creates or enhances a mood, gives visual clues to the course of events, and can even help define pockets of space. The overall brightness of the room can change over the course of the day, but should always be relaxed, never stark, neither too bright nor too dim. Use ambient daylight, overhead lights, and wall sconces to regulate an underlying light level. Dreary overhead fluorescent lights can be dressed up.

OPPOSITE: *The spice added to your table setting need not be limited to what's found in the salt and pepper shakers—rental companies can provide service pieces for the table to suit any style.*

ABOVE: *Clusters of hyacinth and delphinium are grouped in individual bud vases to add the finishing touches to the tabletops.*

Supplemental decorative light can be added in the form of galvanized lanterns, candelabras, votives and tea lights, beaded candle lamps, tapers in candlesticks, pillar candles, strings of tiny fairy lights, festive paper lanterns, hurricane lamps, tiki torches, citronella candles, luminaries, floor lamps—basically anything you can think of. And remember how great everyone looks in candlelight. Spotlights and uplights focus attention on a particular area for visual interest and drama, and battery-operated floodlights beneath the tables create an ethereal glow through the tablecloths. Guests should not have to squint to see their food during the meal, but dim the lights as the celebration progresses toward the dancing section of the party.

ABOVE: *Glass lanterns dot the night sky and light the paths for guests at this outdoor tented affair. A staff member should check the candles during the reception and replace any that are running low.*

OPPOSITE: *Decorative lanterns in varying shapes, sizes, and colors create a visual smorgasbord in the cocktail area at this party. Lanterns can be illuminated with battery-operated lights or strung along electrical wiring wrapped around the tree limbs. Once the sun goes down, the wires will not be visible.*

## Festive Features

*J*azz up your reception with decorative touches throughout the area. A marble column with a magnificent floral arrangement will be a conversation piece. Tall bamboo poles can be inserted into the ground or attached to tent poles to form a natural holder for a floral spray at the top. Create an intimate area where guests can go for a quiet, more private moment. Don't forget that the common spaces—entrances, hallways, and restrooms—will all look more festive with decorative seasonal details.

# Autumn

Mother Nature begins her fall fashion show and everyone's invited. This year, like every year, color is in! As the leaves make their final wardrobe change before the season is over, the earth comes alive with a golden glow that seems to retain all the warmth left from summer's end—well, visually at least, but there's a nip in the air and the wind is picking up, and just about now you're wondering if it's too early to light a fire in the hearth.

Formal or informal, the autumn wedding is steeped in rich images. Treat your guests to texture: this is a transitional season, and almost anything goes. Echo the earth's abundance with color, fabrics, and of course cuisine. Comfort food is a natural fit, and the harvest will provide everything your chef needs for your wedding feast. This is a time for gathering, for preparing for the future, and for celebrating. So gather those dear to you as you take a step into your future, and rejoice in all that autumn has to offer for your seasonal wedding.

## Love in the Vineyard

A beautiful drive through the picturesque countryside sets the stage. As you draw closer, colorful flags in burgundy, purple, and green point the way through winding back roads. By the time the guests find their way to this charming little vineyard, they are already in the mood for a wine lover's celebration. This is wine country, and it is the height of the season. There will be no need for a backup plan today—the weather couldn't be more cooperative. Temperate and bright, this early fall day is just what you wished for, and the festivities will unfold outdoors as hoped.

All of the wines that will be served today are produced at this vineyard, and everyone is in for a treat. Guests are greeted with a choice of sparkling wine or sparkling water, accompanied by figs wrapped in prosciutto and dates stuffed with chorizo and wrapped in bacon. Everyone takes a seat when it's time for the ceremony. The splendor of the outdoor setting needs little embellishment, but a few charming touches have been added to set the scene. Each aisle chair has a miniature bouquet

of dahlias, green viburnum, and cascading champagne grapes. Today, bride and groom will wed under a grape arbor peppered with autum flowers, all reflecting the emerging palette—burgundy, purple, green…the color of grapes.

After offering congratulations in the receiving line, guests head toward the music and the wine-and-cheese buffet. For the adventurous, flights of wine have been set for a real wine-tasting experience. Others can just choose a favorite and stick to it. The bountiful table is lush with piles of colorful fruits and vegetables, an edible still life forming the fare that will start the festivities. Nibble on such fruits as apples, pears, melons, figs, and, of course, grapes, or crostini and focaccia if you are ready for something heartier. Hollowed-out cabbages house dips and spreads for crudités and black bread. Pair them with pâté or your favorite cheese. There are so many to choose from: chèvre, Camembert, peppered Brie, smoked Gouda, Jarlsberg, Bucheron, and even a savory cheese "cake" in the shape of a tiered wedding cake, complete with salmon rosettes and fernlike sprigs of dill. The junior bridesmaid, in her celadon

dress, approaches with the guest book in hand. For this event, a wine-tasting notebook has been chosen to record wishes and wisdom for the couple.

The dinner tables are simple and elegant. Champagne-colored damask tablecloths brush the ground and provide a neutral background. A burgundy napkin of slub silk is reined in by a grapevine ring and a cluster of champagne grapes. The compote centerpiece sits above the table surface, overflowing with sugared grapes—different varieties on different tables—and bold dahlias scattered throughout. Table numbers are crafted of grapevines twisted into the proper shapes and simply leaned against the centerpiece. A profusion of wine glasses adds sparkle and indicates that you had better pace yourself throughout the meal. Each wine has been handpicked to go perfectly with its course, starting with a light, fruity white and progressing with the meal toward a full-bodied red. Even the cake upholds the winery motif: three luscious tiers of the palest green buttercream, with sugared champagne grapes oozing over each tier from twining chocolate vines. Slices are served with a selection of mousses—white chocolate, hazelnut, and apricot. At the end of the evening, each guest receives a personalized wine stopper with the date inscribed on it. It is a very good year indeed.

ABOVE: *Sea scallops are topped with a dollop of frothy milk foam and served elegantly on shells as a first course.*

OPPOSITE: *The spirit of the season is captured in this simple centerpiece. A pumpkin topped with a French-wired bow sits atop a wreath of straw and dried flowers.*

## The Barnyard Dance

From the moment the invitation arrives, the tone for this wedding is clear: rustic elegance. A base sheet of flecked handmade paper in an understated yellow peeks through beneath a vellum overlay, and on the upper sheet, the calligraphed invitation is written in a vibrant italic hand. The two sheets are held together with raffia, and a twig serves as a button to keep them in place. An unusual choice, but the effect is stunning. This wedding promises to be no ordinary occurrence.

The autumn leaves are at the height of their performance, and the weathered wood of the historic barn adds a layer of texture to its surroundings. Although darkness comes earlier these days, the event gets under way before daylight retires for the evening. The ceremony is set outdoors in a clearing in the trees. Rows of weather-worn benches form a circle around the altar, and the path is transformed into an aisle by a thick layer of leaves and petals—natural-looking yet placed there for this occasion. On either side, terra-cotta pots of tall sunflowers look like natural topiaries. The stems of the sunflowers are clustered together and laced with organza ribbon, their heads erupting from above a perky bow at the top of the stems. The bridesmaids, in chocolate brown, carry bouquets composed only of sunflowers, which stand out brightly against their dresses. The bride is bewitching in her free-flowing gown. The medieval sleeves are fitted to the elbow, then open out around her hands and trail down behind her arms,

almost touching the ground. Her long hair is swept up, accented with tiny flowers and sparkling crystal jewels here and there, and a cluster of flowers at the nape of her neck anchors a wisp of gossamer veil, which reaches to her shoulders. She also carries sunflowers, combined with spiky stalks of wheat and soft Queen Anne's lace in a full, constructed bouquet. Her groom has a bold sunflower boutonniere. They keep the ceremony short, as night is approaching and there is a chill in the air.

The barn is aglow in candlelight. At the entrance, two "trees" created from branches are anchored in aged terra-cotta pots flecked with gold leaf. One is full with paper leaves of scarlet and copper and golden yellow, each bearing the name and table number of a guest. This tree follows nature's pattern, losing its leaves one by one as each guest plucks their appropriate seating card from a branch. The other tree has the opposite effect: starting out almost bare, with a pile of blank paper leaves at its base, it looks like it is at the end of the season. But a beautifully calligraphed note instructs guests to use the leaves to write a note to the bride and groom and hang it on the tree; so as the evening progresses, one tree loses its leaves while the other fills with the colors of the season and warm wishes. High above, iron chandeliers intertwined with branches illuminate dark wood rafters that lead the eye around the room. Round tables are set with short squares of thick, leaf-patterned ecru lace, their points hanging over the sides of the table halfway to the floor. The darker cloth beneath extends to the floor on its own, and when you get close, you are surprised to see it is made of burlap, refined for the evening's repast by its elegant overlay. The napkins repeat this unexpected fabric: burlap on one side, a thick ecru low-luster satin on the other.

OPPOSITE: *This bride wears a chapel length veil with blusher to complete her ballgown's silhouette.*

ABOVE: *An autumn leaf and small sprig of pepperberries are fixed to the napkin with an organza bow. Adding interest to the napkins helps fill out the guest tables at a buffet reception, when the table will not be set with dishes.*

Everywhere the eye rests, the room is filled with layer upon layer of visual festive treats. Autumn leaves, bittersweet, seeded eucalyptus, sunflowers, and a cornucopia of cascading fruits and grains in different combinations highlight areas with sculptural effects. Pumpkins and apples are stacked in tumbling piles on bales of hay, with Indian corn and gourds as accents. Miniature pumpkins and sunflower heads have been carved out to hold tea lights. Candelabras and candlesticks are dressed with twining bittersweet; eclectic and harmonious, they fill the space with an intimate radiance. The bar is a distressed-wood trestle table. Its rustic quality makes it perfect for the surroundings, and the beauty of the wood is too magnificent to hide. The smell of hot, spiced ciders—pear and apple—perfumes the air. Glasses are raised as the best man finishes his eloquent toast. The eight-piece band strikes up the next song as a squadron of formally dressed waiters sweep into the room with the first course. This is no ordinary barn dance.

ABOVE: *A bed of moss adds earthy appeal to this interesting twig foundation. Baby carrot and duck prosciutto bundles are placed on galax leaves to separate them from the serving tray.*

OPPOSITE: *Dried wheat and ornamental grasses are distinctive alternatives to flowers. Here, a handful are tied with an opulent satin bow and perched on a windowsill to add an element of harvest reward at this autumn wedding.*

# Accents of Autumn

∽ Press fall leaves of many colors and shapes, then arrange them on your reception tablecloths with an organza overlay on top.

∽ Jazz up your centerpiece with pears, mushrooms, nuts, or colorful gourds. Use potted mums for an economical centerpiece and cover the containers with moss.

∽ Dried flowers are appropriate accents for fall.

∽ Flowering cabbages are a fall phenomenon. Big and blowsy, they add impact and make a sizable impression. You can also use the miniature ones for floral emphasis.

∽ Frozen grapes are a delicious way to chill a drink.

∽ Serve a tiered pumpkin cheesecake instead of a traditional wedding cake.

∽ Use a cluster of lady apples to prop up a place card.

∽ Use miniature pumpkins and gourds as containers for individual flower arrangements at your guests' place settings.

∽ Antique tools add rustic charm to an autumn event.

∽ If fall leaves aren't available in your area, create your own by cutting leaf shapes from organdy, velvet, or colored vellum.

∽ For a touch of whimsy, have your cake crafted to look like a stack of hay bales.

∽ The cornucopia is an apt symbol for autumn. Use it as a container on a buffet table as part of a centerpiece, or even as a cake topper.

∽ Build your bouquet of wild grasses, wheat, straw, hay, soft rushes, and unusually shaped pods.

# Best Dressed

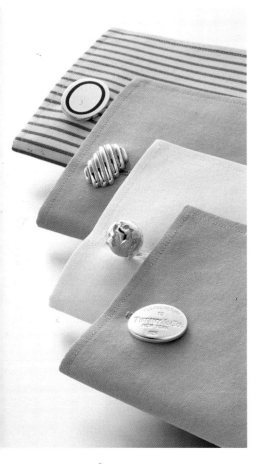

The music pauses, the first notes of the bridal march peal triumphantly, and all eyes turn toward the entrance. The much-anticipated appearance of the bride in all her finery has arrived, and this is the fairy-tale moment she has dreamed of throughout all the planning. There is more eager curiosity about the bride's choice of wedding gown than about any other part of the celebration. Surrounded by a sea of shimmering organza or soft trailing chiffon, she glides down the aisle, carried by the distinction of this special garment, worn on this most unique day. She presents herself to the groom and guests for admiration, feeling every bit the queen for a day.

The wedding dress is magical. From the time we are young children, we are told tales of princesses dressed in gowns such as this who live happily ever after. We have dreamed of this one day in our twenty-first-century lives, when we too can clothe ourselves in a garment of such romance, grandeur, and craftsmanship that bespeaks a ceremonial way of life in times past. And even though tastes may change, even if the flouncy ball gown no longer fits your idea of perfection, the significance of the wedding dress remains. It is likely that more thought and more expense will be given to this one garment than any other you will ever wear. Shape, style, and even color can be combined in endless variety, but when you finally slip on the dress that makes you happy, that makes you feel like a bride, you will know that your search is over.

Bride and groom set the tone for the attire of the rest of the wedding party and the guests. It is perfectly acceptable for the couple to be clad a bit more formally than everyone else, but they should not look so different as to be incongruous. By traditional etiquette, there is a code of proper attire depending on the time of day and level of formality of the event. For bride and bridesmaids, there's a lot of leeway in choosing garments and accessories to fit within these boundaries. For example, a ball gown can be worn at any event, with variables such as the fabric of the dress, the length of the train, and the degree of the embellishment altering the basic silhouette and giving the garment its

ABOVE: *This groom finds his top hat useful in lieu of an umbrella in the shower they encounter after the ceremony.*

personality. For men, the guidelines are more clear-cut, with highly specific garments worn to suit the occasion. As with any "rule" of etiquette, though this code is designed to make life simpler, not more complex; toward that end, it may be adapted to suit modern sensibilities. For instance, one time it was unheard of to wear a tuxedo before 6 P.M., yet nowadays it is a common occurrence. Choose clothing and accessories for yourself, your groom, and the wedding party based on your own sense of what is appropriate for your affair.

## Of a Fashion

Before you shop, do your homework. Look through bridal magazines and wedding books to see what is current in wedding gowns, which styles you like, and the fabrics and trimmings that you would choose. The Internet is a great resource for your research. Many designers maintain a website that shows their current lines and gives information about local shops that carry their garments. There are other sites completely devoted to weddings, and some have thousands of photographs of gowns for you to look at. Next, shop early and shop often! When purchasing your wedding gown, give yourself plenty of time. You may adore the first dress you try on (lucky you!), but it is more likely that you will have to try on many gowns before you reach a decision, requiring several trips to different stores. Once ordered, a traditional gown can take as long as eight months to be made to order by the manufacturer. Then there is a flurry of fittings as the "raw" gown shipped from the manufacturer generally needs alteration and may require one to three visits to the seamstress before it fits you to a tee.

Make an appointment at a bridal salon and bring only one or two others with you. Wear suitable undergarments (such as a strapless bra and pantyhose) and bring along any accessories that you may have already chosen. Bring a few pictures of your favorite gowns to show the salesperson what you like. Tell her the style and formality of the wedding (you'll need to know this before choosing a dress), the wedding date (many brides pad this by a few weeks to a month in case of delays), the time of day that the wedding will be held, and your budget. Don't be disappointed if the shop doesn't carry a sample of the dress of your dreams. It would be impossible for any salon to have every dress on hand—there are literally thousands of bridal gowns available. But giving your salesperson a clear understanding of your taste will allow her to make selections that fit your criteria. She may even suggest something completely different; don't discount such a recommendation. She is an expert in this field and has helped numerous brides find the perfect dress. Based on her assessment of your taste and body type, she may know that

ABOVE: *Your gown becomes a garden of earthly delights when a sheer floral fabric is used as the outer layer, as on this darling dress. The deeply scooped neckline and demure gloves finish the garden-party presentation.*

a particular dress you have not considered might be just what you are looking for. Countless brides report that the dress of their dreams was something they never thought would have looked good on them or that they never considered as being their style. Be open to the experience.

Once you have chosen the dress, the store will take your measurements and draw up your order. Read the order form carefully. Check that everything seems accurate—including the manufacturer number, size, and description of the dress—and make sure

**brush:** gown barely sweeps the floor

**floor:** dress rests just above the floor, perhaps one-half to one inch (12.5 to 25mm)`

**ballet:** hemline is ankle-length; great for an outdoor wedding

**tea length:** hemline falls below midcalf but above ankle

**knee:** just above, just below, or middle

**mini:** hemline is several inches above the knee; may be worn with a detachable train or overskirt

**cathedral:** train falls three yards (2.7m) from the waist, with twenty-two inches (56cm) or more positioned on the floor; appropriate for a very formal wedding

**chapel:** falls four feet (1.2m) from the waist, with twelve to eighteen inches (30.5 to 46cm) positioned on the floor; appropriate for formal and semiformal events

**sweep:** the shortest train; falls about six inches (15cm) onto the floor

**Watteau:** train falls from the shoulders rather than the waist

that all fees and dates are outlined, including alteration fees (which are rarely included in the cost of the gown). Understand that once you place the deposit (which can be a hefty one-third to one-half of the cost of the gown), the dress is yours. Bridal gowns are usually not returnable or exchangeable. If you don't pay the balance and take the dress, most stores will not refund your deposit. Try to pay by credit card, as it offers you some protection in case of a dispute later on.

The silhouette of a wedding dress describes its basic shape. The sleeves, neckline, waistline, hem, and train, as well as a dizzying array of fabrics and trims, modify the silhouette. Using embellishments with lace, pearls, crystals, beads, sequins, braids, gemstones, embroidery, ribbons, or flowers, will change the overall look of a dress dramatically. In addition, body shape plays an important role in how a dress will look. Similar silhouettes can vary greatly from gown to gown, so don't assume you can't wear a particular style simply because one or two dresses did not look flattering on you. The basic silhouettes are:

**Ball gown:** A tight-fitting bodice with a full, bell-shaped skirt. The waistline may be either natural or dropped, and can be rounded or come to a V-shaped point in the front (basque waist). The tight waist and voluminous skirt can have a very slimming effect, particularly with a basque waistline.

**A-line:** A smooth line from head to toe that gradually widens below the hips. The princess cut is also an A-line design, with parallel seams running vertically from the shoulder to the bottom of a flared skirt. There is no waist in this type of dress. The gentle lines of these cuts are flattering on every figure.

**Empire:** A high waist that sits right under the bustline, with a narrow skirt that falls straight to the floor and has no emphasis at the waistline. This classic shape emphasizes the bust, camouflages love handles, and is very comfortable to wear.

**Sheath:** A narrow, form-fitting style with or without a waistline. A detachable train or overskirt can be added for the ceremony. The mermaid style, which widens below the knee, is a variation of the sheath. This contemporary design looks great on a slender bride.

**Suit:** Although not a silhouette per se, the wedding suit is a style worth mentioning. This ensemble features a dress, skirt, or pants (of any length or shape) paired with a matching

jacket or coat. Very progressive, this chic, tailored look can be as sleek or as dressy as you want, and the jacket can even have a train built into it. By varying the shape of the skirt and the length of the jacket, anyone can find a flattering suit style.

By creating a frame for your face, the neckline of your dress is one of the main design features that define it. There are many styles to choose from: off-the-shoulder, halter, scoop (or round), square, strapless, and V neck are all styles we are familiar with. The portrait collar is open at the neckline and may extend off the shoulder slightly, looking almost like a small stole gathered in front at the bustline. The jewel neck has a high, round line that sits at the base of your neck without a collar or binding. The bateau (also called Sabrina) is a boat neck, with a shallow curve or straight line that sweeps across the collarbone from shoulder to shoulder. The band collar is a high, fitted collar that covers part of the neck. The sweetheart is an open neckline that widens from shoulder to chest, then forms a rounded heart shape ending in a point. Décolletage refers to a very open, plunging V that shows off cleavage to dramatic effect. The Queen Anne has an upright collar that comes high up on the back of the neck and is open in front, with the neckline opening to a sweetheart shape. An illusion neckline has a layered effect; the bottom layer may be strapless or have a scoop neck, while the top layer has a jewel neck or band collar and is made of sheer net, tulle, or chiffon.

Sleeves also come in a wide variety of forms, many of which have fallen out of favor in current fashion. Choices range from no sleeve at all (sleeveless, strapless, or spaghetti straps) to simple designs such as cap sleeves, short sleeves, three-quarter sleeves, and long fitted sleeves. A long sleeve may end in a blunt hem, a pointed V, or even a ruffle. More elaborate sleeves include the puffed sleeve; the leg-of-mutton or gigot, which begins in a

PAGE 83: *A modified Watteau train cascades from the top of this strapless gown. Made of the same fabric as the ball gown's overskirt, it features sequins that shimmer daintily in the light.*

ABOVE: *Here, the A-line silhouette, flattering on every figure, is executed in flowing fabrics. The bride chose a sexy spaghetti strap with slight sweetheart shaping at the neckline. The bateau neckline of each attendant's gown is accessorized with a silk flower choker.*

## Buyer's Choice

There are many alternatives to ordering a wedding dress.

**Purchase a bridal salon sample:** If the gown seems to be in good condition or needs only minor repairs or cleaning, you may be able to get a designer gown at a considerable discount.

**Rent a gown or costume:** There are rental shops that specialize in wedding gowns, as well as costume shops that carry period garments that would be quiet wonderful.

**Purchase a used gown:** Certain consignment shops specialize in the sale of wedding clothing. Internet auction sites and antique clothing stores are also wonderful sources.

**Wear an heirloom gown:** If you're lucky enough to have your mother's or grandmother's wedding dress and like the style, this is a lovely tradition.

LEFT: *This bride wears a spray of cut flowers in her hair and at the waistline of her dress to match her bouquet. Your mother may choose to wear a neutral color, or a color to match or coordinate with the wedding colors.*

# Material Girl

## Summer

The summer wedding dress glorifies the freedom of this time of year. A silk charmeuse slip dress is luxurious and very trendy. Cotton piqué and linen are light, breathable fabrics. A tulle ball skirt works at any time of year, but soft organza, crisp organdy, or dotted Swiss are perfect for a garden wedding. Bare is beautiful… choose an open neckline with a bolero or wrap to cover up for a religious ceremony. Add a touch of color with beautiful embroidery. Cap sleeves, short sleeves, a strapless dress, or a sleeve of lace or netting will keep you comfortable. Think twice about a train for an outdoor wedding: dragging your beautiful white dress over outdoor terrain may take a toll even before the ceremony is over.

## Autumn

Silk's many finishes and its natural properties to breathe make it a wonderful fabric year-round, but especially during months when the weather could turn chilly. For the fall, go with into a shantung or dupioni, with its raw, nubby texture, and low luster. Your glossy satin dress can have a bit more weight to it than a satin used in warmer months. Choose a graceful A-line covered in Venise lace with a sweep train coyly brushing the floor. Rich damask or jacquard, with a hint of metallic thread woven into the pattern, is luxurious when translated into any silhouette. Ivory melds well with the colors of autumn. A three-quarter sleeve keeps you snug while fending off the advances of winter.

## Winter

There's no doubt that velvet is the winter fabric; picture yourself in a lavish gown of the softest white velvet wrapped in a cape of the deepest royal blue, and be prepared to be cuddled by everyone. Winter weddings naturally gravitate toward the formal, with sumptuous fabrics and lots of fine beading. Brocade, a heavy cloth with pattern woven into it, is right at home in the cold months. Faux fur trim shows the animal lover in you and adds a touch of retro charm. If the bright jewel colors of Christmastime are not your thing, choose a gown of the palest ice blue and see if anyone notices the color.

## Spring

An elegant empire gown of softly draped chiffon bespeaks the gentility of neoclassic style, perfect for the buoyancy of spring. Rum pink is a delicious color for this time of year…rosy and fresh in any fabric. Crepe de chine and delicate lace are light and lovely, or if something more substantial is your style, a perky faille ball skirt topped by a lightweight sweater set really makes a statement—especially when bare shoulders are the case with a strapless dress. Or add a fitted illusion sleeve of the sheerest net for almost invisible protection against the unpredictable weather.

full puff at the shoulder and is gathered just above the elbow, then finished with a fitted sleeve; the bishop, which is narrow at the top of the sleeve and gradually widens to a full gathered puff at the wrist, sometimes with a cuff; and the bell sleeve, which is narrow at the top and gradually widens to a full, open bottom.

## Finishing Touches

When it comes to wedding attire, accessories are the icing on the cake. They complement and complete your outfit, highlight choice features, and move the gaze around from head to toe to create a "whole." You might select a headpiece, a veil, gloves, a purse, shoes, jewelry, lingerie, and a wrap—or any part thereof—to complete your wedding ensemble. Unless you are planning to wear your grandmother's gloves or the ruby earrings that your fiancé gave you on Valentine's Day, choose your dress first, then let that decision drive your accessories. Once your dress is selected, concentrate on purchasing your lingerie and shoes next. You will need to have them with you for your first fitting so that your dress can be tailored and hemmed perfectly. When shopping for your other accessories, wear a shirt that has a neckline and sleeves similar to your gown's bodice, if possible.

Comfort is key for bridal shoes. You will be on your feet for hours on end, taking photos, dancing, and visiting with all your guests. Your shoes should offer support and balance and should fit securely without squeezing your feet. Some brides buy shoes half a size larger than normal—with all that activity, feet have a tendency to swell. Choose a heel of only one or two inches (2.5 or 5cm) for maximum comfort. Avoid stilettos if your wedding is outside on grass or ground, unless it is your intention to aerate the lawn with your heels during your walk down the aisle.

Evening shoes are exquisite. While a closed pump is the most formal, you may opt for an airy sandal or slingback for an open look. These come in beautiful fabrics such as silk, satin, peau de soie, velvet, and brocade (leather and suede shoes are considered too casual). They can be decorated with embroidery, lace, beads, silk flowers, bows, or pearls; left unadorned; embellished with jeweled shoe clips or fresh flowers; or customized to match the trim on your dress. Take along a swatch from your gown

OPPOSITE: *Savor every moment of your wedding day. Dressing with your bridesmaids can be a cherished experience. Take a moment to take it all in and toast your groom, but be careful not to overindulge.*

ABOVE: *Accessories hone your ensemble to perfection. This bride chose elbow-length sheer gloves and an embroidered purse, then added a touch of sparkle with a tiara.*

*A simple wrap of a sheer fabric, such as organza, organdy, or chiffon, is a romantic companion to any wedding gown. The hem is painstakingly rolled at the edges for a fine finish.*

to coordinate the two fabrics. White or ivory are the conventional colors, of course, and shoes can be dyed to match the exact hue of your dress. An adorable option is to select shoes to represent your "something blue." Robin's egg or a pale frost blue shoe is a delightful surprise when your skirt is demurely lifted during the garter toss or a traditional ethnic dance. Break in your shoes before the wedding day by wearing them around the house often, but be sure to keep them in immaculate condition. For traction on slippery dance floors, scuff the bottom of the heels and soles gently with fine sandpaper.

The combination of headpiece and veil is often the final touch that makes a woman feel like a bride. You may choose to wear one without the other or forgo headgear completely, but the diversity of styles available is vast, and a stunning headpiece enhances and finishes your wedding ensemble. As a general rule, your headpiece and gown should be well balanced. If your dress is very ornate, choose a simpler headpiece and veil so that they don't compete with the gown. When selecting your headpiece, try to imagine how you want to wear your hair. Also consider the conditions surrounding your wedding...a wide-brimmed hat will obscure your face from view, makes hugging and kissing difficult, and could be unruly on a windy day. A smaller hat or cap will be more manageable. Enchanting tiaras and crowns made of crystals, pearls, faux gemstones, and lustrous metals are extremely popular today. Combs are also a great choice. Or perhaps a simple headband, jeweled barrette, or bow is more to your liking. Fresh flowers are a lovely option, whether attached to a headpiece, made into a delicate spray or wreath, or interwoven directly into your hairstyle.

The veil is one of the most distinct symbols of the wedding costume. An ethereal wisp of netting, the veil is usually made of tulle or illusion lace. You might choose a veil with an unfinished edge or a rolled edge in satin or silk, or finished with ribbon or lace. The veil may be embellished with pearls, crystals, embroidery, or lace designs to match your dress, or it may be kept pristinely unadorned. It might be sewn to your headpiece or attached with snaps, hooks, or Velcro for easy removal at the beginning of the reception. If you choose to wear your veil throughout the festivities, as is sometimes the case with a flyaway or fingertip veil attached at the nape of the neck, make sure it is fastened securely. Every time someone embraces you or dances with you, they will accidentally tug at your veil. When trying on your dress, try veils of different lengths and fullnesses in order to select a style that offers proportion and balance.

The blusher is the chin-length veil that is worn over the face as you walk down the aisle. Your father or groom will lift it to the back of your head. Most second-time brides forgo the blusher. The fingertip veil, between waist and fingertip length, is perfect for almost any dress—the exception being an extremely formal gown. The flyaway is a multi-

ABOVE: *A floral accompaniment of gardenias and stephanotis will remain in place during the reception, after the mantilla-type veil is removed. White pearls are the classic bridal accessory, paired here with diamonds for a timeless look.*

layer, shoulder-length veil. Ballet or waltz length comes just above the ankle. As with train lengths, the sweep brushes the floor, the chapel pools two and a half yards (2.3m) from the headpiece, and the cathedral trails three and a half yards (3.2m) from the headpiece. A mantilla is often made of lace and is draped directly on the head without a headpiece, enveloping the bride.

Your wedding jewelry should be simple, elegant, and choice. It must complement your dress and headpiece, not take attention away from them. The more elaborate the dress, the daintier the jewelry. It is not necessary to wear a full suite of jewels. Sometimes a beautiful pair of earrings is all that is required to frame your face. Pearls are the

## Isn't She Lovely?

The best look for a bride on her wedding day is an unaffected one. Makeup should be subtle, enhancing your features and coloring rather than overwhelming them. Makeup, properly applied, will define your face in photographs while remaining natural up close and personal. A good foundation is invisible and will even out skin tones. A thin line of eyeliner defines lids, but does not look good on everyone. Shadow should be subtle and soft, or skip it altogether. Mascara lengthens and frames your eyes. Use a lip liner to line and fill in your lips, then apply lipstick on top for an even, long-lasting look. A dusting of powder will keep everything in place for hours. Avoid makeup with a lot of shine, as it doesn't photograph well.

Keep your wedding-day hairstyle simple, classic, and all about you. An updo is elegant and will hold its shape all day with a minimum of fussing—a chignon, French knot, or bun will allow everyone to see you clearly and show off your jewelry and headpiece. If you are inclined to wear your hair down, consider sweeping the front away from your face, and be prepared to touch it up with comb and hairspray throughout the day to keep it looking fresh. Short hair is liberating at a wedding and looks stunning with a tiara or headband. Have a trial run of your hairstyle with the headpiece several weeks before the wedding, and take a photograph when you get it just right. Hair should be colored and trimmed about a week before the wedding. Don't make any big changes close to the date, however. Experimenting with a new color or a drastically different cut is courting disaster as it may not work out to your liking.

Select hair or makeup styles that reflect your personality. On your wedding day, you want to look like a dolled-up version of you, not someone your guests or your groom won't recognize. Don't rush yourself. Allow several hours for hair, makeup, and dressing at a leisurely pace. Remember, this is a day to cherish—avoid stress by setting aside plenty of time to pamper and primp yourself.

traditional preference for many brides, but your choice should be based on the style and trimming on your gown and headdress. A borrowed family bracelet or an heirloom necklace adds great significance to this part of your costume. Avoid wearing many rings as it may detract from the significance of your wedding band—you may switch your engagement ring to your right hand during the ceremony.

Other accessories may be chosen to complete your outfit. A purse may be one item too many for you to keep track of, but if you don't want to rely on someone else to carry your lipstick, there are dainty bags that will harmonize perfectly with your ensemble. Handbags can be as elaborately decorated and customized as any other part of your wedding attire. Embroidered accents from your gown, veil, or wrap can be echoed in your purse to unify your overall look.

Gloves are a refined finishing touch with many dresses. Short gloves add a charming, old-fashioned dash to almost any sleeve length. Elbow- or opera-length gloves are elegant with a sleeveless or strapless gown. Gloves are made in many fabrics and trimmings, so the style can be matched perfectly to the rest of what you are wearing. Slip your left glove off for the exchange of rings, or open the seam in the ring finger of the glove to slip your finger out at the proper moment. After the ceremony, gloves should be taken off for the receiving line and during the meal.

In any season, the bride should consider completing her wedding wardrobe with a wrap or a shawl which can be made with a number of fine fabrics. A summery tuft of tulle clasped with a brooch that matches your tiara, a delicately draped length of beaded chiffon, or a dramatic cape or stole for colder climates will provide fashionable comfort either outdoors or in an air-conditioned room.

ABOVE: *A pair of rhinestone and pearl earrings dangle playfully from these peau de soie sandals. Although these jewels are meant to adorn the ears, not the heels, of this bride, rhinestone clips can be added to doll up plain shoes if you wish.*

## Faithful Friends

The much-maligned bridesmaid's dress has become a cliché of bad taste in our culture, but the days of over-the-top puffy confections of cheesy fabric and too much trim are over. Today's tastes run toward the sophisticated, the elegant, and even the practical. Although you can't please all of the people all of the time, selecting garments for your attendants should be handled diplomatically.

Bridesmaids' dresses should match the style and spirit of the event and coordinate well with your attire. Typically, gowns are made to order to attendants' measurements, just as yours is, and can take anywhere from six weeks to four months to arrive (plus additional time for fittings). Gowns should all be ordered from one place at the same time, as garments made from different dye lots will show slight differences in color. As soon as you have selected your gown, begin looking for theirs. Take along your maid or matron of honor and perhaps one of the maids; shopping with more than that at one time may be cumbersome. Be sensitive to their varying body types and budgets—most attendants purchase their own apparel, so the thoughtful bride will choose dresses that will not be a financial burden to them. They will appreciate it if you select styles that are flattering,

ABOVE: *This simple cut will look good on many different figure types. The dropped waist is flattering, the full skirt hides a multitude of sins, and the crisp fabric is softened by the contrasting lace top.*

modern, and well made, increasing their chances of wearing the garment again.

The conventional look is to have all attendants dress alike. However, sometimes the maid of honor may have a distinguishing feature about her attire—such as the same dress in a coordinating color, a different dress in the same color, or the same dress with a different sleeve or embellishment.

More brides today ignore convention and choose a creative, nontraditional option for their attendants' attire, and their bridesmaids are thanking them for it. Select a single

# Underneath It All

Petticoats, slips, and lingerie will greatly affect the line of your garment. Many dresses have crinolines, slips, and linings built into them, yet may still need an added underskirt for extra lift or definition. When you are shopping for your dress, try on petticoats of varying stiffness and volume to see what looks best under your dress. You may be able to purchase the petticoat directly from the bridal salon, or ask for recommendations about where to shop.

Purchase undergarments shortly before your first fitting; you can even buy several styles to see which works best with your dress and then return the rejects (make sure you keep the sales receipts). Depending on the dress's bodice, neckline, and sleeves, you'll probably need special lingerie—a strapless bra, bustier, or corset. Pantyhose should be sheer, in a natural color or with a soft white, taupe, or pink cast, depending on the color of your dress. It's a good idea to purchase an extra pair of stockings in case of tears. And don't forget your garter: even if you don't intend to do the traditional toss, wearing a delicately ruffled garter on your leg is a lovely custom.

---

designer, fabric, and color, and let the attendants choose dresses in styles that suit them. Many designers (and department stores) are showing separates that can be mixed and matched in the same fabrics and colors to create a custom and coordinated look for each attendant. A common skirt for all in a flattering cut can be paired with a top of their own choosing in an easy-to-match color, such as black or white. For the free-spirited bride, surprise yourself by giving your attendants an apparel assignment—allow each to select her own black cocktail suit or floor-length dress in navy blue—and delight in watching their choices blend together harmoniously on your wedding day.

As with their garments, you can have as much or as little control over your attendants' accessories as you wish. If you like a uniform appearance, let each choose her own comfortable shoes in the same neutral color or have shoes dyed to match the gowns.

As a gift to thank them for their support, many brides select jewelry for their attendants to wear at the wedding. On the other hand, a diverse but well-coordinated group of attendants is visually exciting and contemporary—certainly an excellent way to inject your wedding with a unique flair. Allowing your individuality and that of your bridesmaids to flourish and shine is a surefire way to avoid the "cookie-cutter" trap.

## The Best Man

And that would be your groom, of course! As far as wedding clothes go, a man's decisions are much more limited than a woman's, but following specific guidelines can be freeing in and of itself. Traditional etiquette dictates that certain garments be worn depending on the time of day and formality of the affair. A very formal morning wedding demands a morning suit, with its long cutaway jacket of gray or black, gray waistcoat, white shirt, and black and gray striped trousers. An ascot or striped four-in-hand tie completes the picture, and the most formal groom should also sport a dove gray top hat, gloves, and spats. The most formal of evening events, beginning after 6 P.M., might call for white tie, also known as full dress. A man looks most elegant in a black tailcoat (left unbuttoned) and black trousers, a white wing-collar shirt, and white piqué vest and bow tie. He would complete the picture with black top hat and white gloves.

At a formal or semiformal daytime wedding, the groom might substitute a stroller (a long black or gray jacket) for the cutaway, to be worn over his striped trousers. For

RIGHT: *A single miniature calla is finished with a springy curl for this sophisticated boutonniere.*

LEFT: *It's not every day that your man gets a chance to indulge himself as well. In a dapper dove gray top hat and walking stick, a groom will feel dressed to the nines.*

the evening formal, he might choose to wear black tie or one of the many styles of tuxedo. A white or ivory dinner jacket is appropriate for an evening wedding in warm weather. A suit is perfect for an informal event, while a blazer and trousers are fine for a casual affair.

Although tradition dictates that the groom and groomsmen be dressed alike, it is nice for the groom to stand out in some way. This might be accomplished with a special boutonniere, a different tie, a colored cummerbund, a vest, beautiful studs and cufflinks, a luxurious white silk scarf, kid gloves, patent leather opera slippers, or black oxfords—any of these elements can help the groom to let his personality shine through. At a semiformal wedding, the groom could sport a white dinner jacket while the groomsmen wear black tuxedos. For an informal event, the groom might don a navy suit while his attendants are dressed in navy blazers and tan trousers. Like the female members of the wedding party, the groomsmen may be asked to wear black tuxedos of their own choosing rather than identical formalwear.

## Smart Style

The pleats of a cummerbund point up.

Wear a boutonniere or a pocket handkerchief, but not both.

Tie and pocket square should not match.

## Treat Her Right

*W*eddings are stressful for all involved, so pamper yourself and your attendants whenever possible. A trip to a day spa with your attendants is a luxurious "girls' day out" ritual. If that doesn't fit your pocketbook, re-create the atmosphere at home with healthy snacks, candles, and music while applying mud packs and doing each other's nails. Make an appointment for you and your attendants to get manicures and pedicures on the day before or morning of the wedding. Don't forget about your groom. Setting aside time to connect and enjoy each other is one of the best things you can do for both of you.

OPPOSITE: *The flower girls take a moment to admire their baskets. Their floor-length, matching dresses are simple and sweet, and mimic the shape of the bride's wedding gown.*

## Fresh Faces

Your youngest attendants will have no trouble getting into the spirit of the event. Children love a wedding, with all its pomp and mysterious rituals. They immediately grasp the dignity of the event and jump into the festivities with gusto. While they can be unpredictable, when they're dressed in their wedding finery and carrying out their appointed duties with the utmost seriousness, they come very close to stealing the show.

Your flower girl's dress should have the same level of formality as the attire of your other attendants. This does not mean it should be a copy of the bridesmaids' dresses, or yours, but it should coordinate. She might wear a dress harmonious in color to that of the adult attendants, in a similar tone or a pastel shade, or a white dress becoming to a small child. Let her have her own identity rather than making her into a miniature bride. Flower girls look especially darling in short, three-quarter- or ballet-length dresses. A floor-length dress is also an option, though this might be awkward for a very young girl. She will be concentrating on the job of sprinkling petals evenly in the aisle; you don't want her to worry about tripping on her dress. She can wear something ethereal or tailored without losing any of her innocence. Tights or anklets with a lace cuff, paired with Mary Janes or nonskid ballet slippers, complete the picture.

While formalwear is available in children's sizes, your ring bearer may look more appropriate in something suited to his age. A white Eton jacket and shorts are charming, as are knickers with a matching jacket. Your little man will look dapper in a blazer and trousers or a suit with a bow tie that matches the wedding colors. Coordinate his ring pillow to the rest of the wedding party with the fabric or ribbons used to secure the rings. A gentlemanly boutonniere, in miniature, lets him know how important he is.

When selecting children's clothing, keep comfort in mind. Fabrics should be soft and breathable, and styles should not be binding or cause them to fuss. Give them the opportunity to break in their dress shoes before the event. Children are less accustomed to wearing fancy clothes, and their garments should in no way restrict them. Make sure they love what they are wearing, and have them dress as close to the starting time as possible so that they look fresh for the ceremony and photographs.

## Chapter Seven
# *Winter*

Snowmen and snow angels, icicles and ice rinks—there's no doubt about it: the cold of winter is packed with pleasure. The world begins to sparkle and shine by the time December rolls around and keeps on going until spring. 'Tis the season to be jolly, and wherever you look, everyone is in a good mood, whether they're hurrying about to get their holiday shopping done, planning New Year's Eve parties, or snuggling in with a cup of tea in a cozy window seat. Good spirits are infectious, and "festive" is the word of the day. In January and February, when the earth is draped in wedding white, a more tranquil atmosphere pervades, with perhaps a bit of celebration withdrawal setting in after the crescendo of activity.

Winter by its nature has a formal flair, deep and rich and layered. Bundle up for the season by wrapping your wedding in extravagance; larger than life fits right in at this time of year. Flowers are a special treat when the earth is bare, so lavish them on your surroundings, your guests, and yourself. Or mix a few precious blooms with more seasonal fare, such as evergreens, juniper, pinecones, and mistletoe. See to it that everything is dressed in its best, and may your winter wedding be merry and bright.

## Home for the Holidays

This wedding is a family affair in every sense of the word. Kindred spirits have offered their special talents to make this the most intimate of nuptials, and each will bestow a piece of themselves to personalize this day. Your youngest sister, the bride, has confided to you that her excitement is heightened by the fact that she has not planned every last detail of this event. Instead in a spirit of collaboration and spontaneity, she has delegated selected details to her loved ones and trusted in their imagination and abilities.

Many surprises are in store for her today, and she will delight in having the same experience as her guests, seeing all the elements coalesce for the first time on her wedding day. One of the groom's

ABOVE: *A pair of matching baskets cradles treasures for two young girls to carry during the ceremony.*

OPPOSITE: *White and gold add buoyancy and elegance to the understated furnishings in this stately room. Although candles are not needed for illumination during the day, they will add an extra bit of sparkle to this room when lit.*

sisters has volunteered to create the centerpieces, another is making the favors, and your husband, a professional photographer, will be recording the day's events on film while your oldest nephew videotapes the event.

Baking is your personal specialty in the family, and today your contribution to the celebration is the wedding cake. You were told only to keep it in the spirit of the Christmas season but to choose your own design. Your labor of love is a tiered confection that tapers gradually to the top. The sides of each layer have been trimmed at an angle, narrower at the top than the bottom, and frosted with a creamy ivory buttercream. Each of the three layers is a different flavor to please all of the family palates. Between each tier you have constructed an almost solid layer of red roses, glittering cranberries, and green ivy, tapered like the tiers to connect them and form a smooth cone from top to bottom. At the top of your edible Christmas tree

you've placed a delicate crystal star, which you hope the bride and groom will hang on their own tree in years to come.

You arrive with anticipation at the couple's new home, where the wedding will take place. Outside, the house is radiant with the glow of icicle lights and winter votives burning within containers of ice set in the snow along the path. A welcoming wreath hangs on the front door, inviting everyone in. Still mostly unfurnished, the house has plenty of room to accommodate the rented tables and chairs necessary for the wedding dinner. Once inside, delicious aromas waft from the kitchen.

You catch sight of the dining area—decked out with your mother's finest china, silver, and crystal—and supplemented with neutral, coordinating pieces from the rental company to stretch her service to accommodate the guest list. Rented ficus trees intertwined with tiny lights fill in the empty corners, and boxwood garlands drape gently over the curtained window sashes. Lush brocade tablecloths sweep the floor, and golden

OPPOSITE: *Red is right at any time of year, but looks particularly dramatic in the white of winter. Match your nail polish to the color of your bouquet to further unify your palette.*

ABOVE: *Rows of red petals contrast with the unadulterated snowy white tiers of this pristine cake.*

ballroom chairs each have a sprig of holly and pine attached to the back with a cranberry-colored bow. On each table, a different grouping of crystal vases surrounds ivory pillar candles of varying heights, while ivy winds its way around containers and candles to tie them together. In one vase there is a tight grouping of red roses, in another a floating candle. Yet another is filled with cranberries and water with a single ivory rose floating on top. Roses, cranberries, ivy…great minds think alike.

You turn the cake over to the caterer and your coat to a member of her staff and join the party where family and friends have gathered in the living room. A waiter offers premium champagne and blini with caviar. For a wedding this exclusive, it is easy to pull out all the stops; a small guest list means each detail can be more lavish and of the finest quality. Every facet has been handpicked or handcrafted, from the invitations (individually rendered by the bride's best friend in the most exquisite calligraphy and wrapped in delicately patterned rice paper) to the wedding bands (designed by the bride and groom and created by an artisan) to the bride's bouquet (a stunning burst of red and white variegated amaryllis, white roses, and paperwhite narcissus lovingly cultivated by the groom's younger sister).

Appropriately, the ceremony will take place in the family room. Bride and groom have chosen to forgo the drama of the grand entrance and are already there, mingling with their loved ones in front of the blazing fireplace. Your sister looks gorgeous in Grandmother's wedding dress, a beaded Chantilly lace sheath from the 1920s. In one corner, next to a seven-foot (2m) Christmas tree, a jazz quartet plays sweetly. When it is time to begin, the bride and groom take their places, surrounded by their friends and family, and speak the vows that they wrote themselves.

The pace for the wedding is leisurely; there is no pressure to perform rigidly scheduled rituals, or to leave at an appointed hour. Throughout the evening, everyone takes a moment to toast the happy couple, share a personal memory, or state their good wishes for bride and groom. This couple wanted their wedding to reflect their unique perspective and uncontrived style. By choosing a location of such significance and getting their loved ones involved in presenting the special touches, they have done just that. This wedding is about lifestyle, personality, history, and sharing. There's no place like home.

## A Winter Wonderland

This wedding has already made an impression: set in a mammoth cathedral in the heart of the city, the ceremony boasted a sense of grandeur that was amplified by the vast space. Ushers greeted the guests at the door and escorted them to their seats. A junior bridesmaid was given the job of handing out programs, and she performed her assignment with the utmost reverence. The programs themselves were simple and elegant—the finest snow white paper engraved with black ink, with delicate snowflakes embossed intermittently on the pages. Bridesmaids, dressed in platinum satin ballroom skirts and white cashmere sweater sets, carried chic velvet muffs affixed with corsages of gardenia. Both flower girl and ring bearer handled their responsibilities perfectly, the latter stopping only long enough to wave to his young cousin seated about midway down the aisle. The bride, dressed in a satin ball gown of impressive proportion, carried a bouquet of distinct shades of white flowers: roses, stephanotis, gardenias, white violets, and snowberries. The bejeweled stephanotis centers sparkle as they catch the light, but there is something more, and as she passes you see that crystal "snowflakes" have been wired into the bouquet.

The ceremony took place hours ago, and some of the out-of-town guests have been passing the time in a hospitality suite at a nearby hotel, recounting tales of bride and groom throughout their lives. Now they're ready for an evening of dining and dancing in a sparkling cityscape, and they won't be disappointed. A penthouse loft offers windows on three of the room's four walls, and the views of the glittering city on a snowy night are

ABOVE: *'Tis the season to utilize your surroundings. Find ways to highlight an area with a spectacular feature. Here, guests are drawn over to a charming conversation area with an incredible view. Some red fabric and small floral arrangements are all that is needed to tie inside and outside together.*

spectacular. Votive candles line the windowsills, mimicking the lights of the city in perfect alignment. White walls are the blank canvas in this room, broken up here and there by the glimmer of tiny fairy lights. Stately white columns wrapped in light climb to meet an elevated ceiling adorned with crystal chandeliers. Everything in this room is white or silver, an homage to winter. Heavy white linen tablecloths are covered with white organza embroidered with a snowflake pattern… subtle, yet darling. Candelabras and votives illuminate each table. Silver-beaded chargers are set beneath white china, and cut crystal catches and reflects the many dancing lights. Silver mint julep cups hold miniature arrangements of white flowers plus table numbers carved from ice. Before they begin to melt, a waiter discreetly whisks the numbers away. A scattering of coarse salt on the tabletop looks like a dusting of snow, and the sparks of the candles skip along the surface.

In one corner, a small birch tree is covered in tiny lights. Beneath it rests an antique sleigh, and guests are placing gifts for the bride and groom in it. A waiter hands you a hot white chocolate with a little kick to it, and you instantly feel warmer. At the bar, a stacked, tiered ice sculpture shaped like a wedding cake provides plenty of ice cold surface area to keep an assortment of designer vodka shots well chilled. Maybe later, but right now the hors d'oeuvre buffet table beckons, with mouthwatering fare such as truffled quail eggs with wasabi caviar, bite-size crepes filled with duck breast and roasted apple conserve, skewers of goat cheese ravioli dripping in sage butter, and roasted cherry tomatoes stuffed with shrimp and lemon basil. You can hardly wait to find out what's for dinner, but the band is starting to play your favorite swing tune, and you head off to find your partner before the dance is over. Formal and fun: that's the formula for a winter wedding.

ABOVE: *This New Year's Eve wedding sparkles and winks everywhere you turn. Building on basic black and white, colored gels take the edge off bright lighting, infusing the setting with an azure glow and dancing off the silver charger, stemware, and beaded silk napkin. A silver-framed place card holder doubles as a favor for guests.*

OPPOSITE: *This bride borrows a jacket on her way into the church on this wintry day. If you plan to wear your heels outside, make sure the paths are cleared.*

ABOVE: *Arrive in style at any time of year. This horse-drawn carriage oozes romance. Like a fairy-tale princess, this bride gets to the ball just in time.*

OPPOSITE: *At the reception, place your bouquet in a visible spot where it will have impact.*

# Winter Whimsy

- Frosty still lifes of sugared fruit make beautiful centerpieces.

- Serve "snowballs" for dessert: round balls of vanilla, almond, or white chocolate sorbet rolled in coconut.

- Add a white feather boa to the hem of your A-line gown.

- In keeping with the season's generosity of spirit, arrange for food leftover from your reception to be delivered to a homeless shelter.

- For a fun favor, give your guests snow globes from the local area, or make your own and include a laminated photo of the two of you and your wedding date.

- Have guests ring jingle bells as you exit the church after the ceremony.

- Decorate your shoes with faux-fur trim.

- Give mittens embroidered with snowflakes as your favors.

- Carry an antique Bible or other appropriate family heirloom, carefully festooned with flowers, instead of a bouquet.

- Use handcrafted glass flowers and artificial beaded fruits in your bouquet.

- Make white chocolate snowflakes for favors.

- Have your bridesmaids carry wreaths or garlands instead of bouquets.

- In a snowy rural area, rent a horse and sleigh to transport you to the ceremony and reception for the day.

- Make glowing snowballs out of roly-poly votives by painting them with white glue and rolling them in faux snow.

- Pinecones with the tips painted with glass glitter are an appropriate seasonal decoration.

- Hang mistletoe in a choice spot on the dance floor and make sure you steal a kiss from your husband every time you pass underneath it.

- Add a touch of red to your celebration to tie it to Christmas or Valentine's Day or to bring good luck in the Chinese New Year.

- Create a twinkling night sky over your dance floor with fairy lights and tulle.

- Ask guests to sing a wintery song instead of clinking glasses if they'd like to see you and your new hubby kiss.

# Decorative Details

ABOVE: *The swirls of the tablecloth are echoed in the decorative script, and the pink and green wedding colors are repeated in the hand-painted flower.*

OPPOSITE: *The wedding cake has become a work of art that defies traditional stereotypes. This whimsical fondant creation can stand up to a hot summer day and will bring a smile to the face of everyone who sees it.*

The hall is booked, the menu is confirmed, your dress is ordered, and your bridesmaids have all accepted. Ceremony scheduled? Check! Table settings chosen? Check! Bouquets and centerpieces ordered? Check, check! You're not quite done, but you've reached the home stretch. Just a few finishing touches remain, and many of these little effects are just what are needed for that extra bit of seasonal panache.

An enormous amount of wedding-planning time is spent thinking about small details that will be seen for only a few moments. Yet when you add up all those details, they create the overall sense of the wedding's style. Some, such as place cards, table numbers, favors, and guest books, will be seen and touched by your guests. Although they may or may not consciously notice the extra "seasoning" you have added, it still makes an impression. And if you have a penchant for detail, you will notice. Since these items will probably be the first things your guests come in contact with—up close and personal—at the reception, the presentation can be as important as the substance.

Your wedding cake is one place where you can really let your imagination soar. Today, wedding cakes are as interesting on the outside as they are on the inside, and finding ways to tie into a seasonal theme is literally a piece of cake! Plan to exhibit it throughout the reception, giving you and your guests plenty of time to enjoy its outer intricacies. The table display should highlight and frame your cake, complementing its design rather than overpowering it.

While not a visual detail, your choice of music can affect the entire event. Music sets the mood at your ceremony, fills in the blanks during cocktails, and creates the tempo at the reception. Working hand in hand with the caterer and the wedding coordinator, the band leader or disc jockey cues the events that take place during the reception, which helps to avoid confusion and keep the pace going.

Hiring a photographer and a videographer will give you a permanent record of the events of the day that will bring you great pleasure in years to come. Countless brides and grooms report that after

long months of planning and organizing, the wedding itself was a blur, over before they knew it. When the whirlwind subsides, these visual records will stir your memories of the day, recording not only the fine points of style that you labored over but the features of a wedding that really count: the people—a dance with Uncle Eugene, the best man's toast, a joke told by your flower girl, or bride and groom in a tender embrace. As time tries to fade your memories, your photographs and video will keep them fresh in your mind, season after season.

ABOVE: *Romance is in full bloom at this afternoon garden event. A diaphanous cloud of gossamer fabric covers the bride and groom's chairs, reigned in with bountiful bouquets tied to the chair backs. The clever design of a three-tier ice sculpture keeps food cool on a hot summer's day.*

## Places, Please

Planning seating arrangements for your guests is a thoughtful and important reception detail. It relieves them of the need to jockey for position when they arrive at the reception and eliminates the possibility of people who may not enjoy each other's company ending up at the same table. You can assign tables only and let guests choose their specific seats or designate both table and seat by putting individual place cards at each setting.

Once all of your responses have arrived, write the name of each individual or couple on index cards, and begin to sort them into groups that make sense. Have a cousins' table, put your work colleagues together, and mingle people with similar interests or age groups. Seat singles at tables with outgoing guests who will engage them in conversation. When you have an arrangement that works, with all guests accounted for and all tables hosting a comfortable number of people, staple each group of cards together. Use the cards as a blueprint for writing out the place cards or to create an alphabetized master list to give to a calligrapher.

When deciding on the floor plan or positioning of the tables, keep in mind that your parents or important family members should be seated close to you near the front of the room. Older guests will appreciate being seated farther away from the band or speakers, where they won't be disturbed by loud music.

Many people prefer round tables at a wedding. It is the most popular choice, and hence you may find more alternatives for table linens and centerpieces. In addition, round tables are easily arranged to create a flow for traffic patterns in the room. Round tables also allow guests the maximum amount of visual contact with other people at their table, which many translate to mean that guests will have access to more people for conversation. Don't feel restricted by this guideline, however. Even with the best intentions, your guests will likely have conversations only with the people in closest proximity to them. Yelling above the music and other people's conversations over a five-foot (1.5m) expanse of tabletop is not conducive to intimate conversation. It is likely that guests sitting across from each other at a round table will exchange only a few words. Rectangular tables, on the other hand, allow guests the same access to two people on either side of them as well as the four across from them. Stacking long banquet tables end to end without break, with guests seated on both sides, is a modern approach to wedding seating that is rapidly gaining in popularity. Either way, your guests will have no trouble

ABOVE: *Lighting really sets the mood in this fabulous location. Candles, spotlights, and uplights do more than illuminate, they radiate. Lights have been used to add drama and call attention to the noteworthy architectural elements of this room.*

finding plenty of people to engage in conversation, so choose the option that best suits your style.

Informing your guests of their seating assignments is a chance to let your creative juices flow. Choose a classic ecru or white card with a thin gold or silver edge, an elegant tent card, or an enveloped escort card, or let your imagination soar. This is a perfect place for introducing seasonal elements.

- Decorate cards with ribbons in your wedding colors, tiny flowers or buds, or embossed or cut-out shapes. Or use metallic or colored ink.
- Cut out appropriate shapes from paper, such as a daisy, snowflake, or leaf, and perch on the edge of a wineglass.
- Write the guest's name on an inner card and the table number on the outside of a small colored vellum envelope. Fill the envelope with petals or seeds.
- Set up your cards on a bed of hydrangea petals, pine needles, colored leaves, or fake snow.
- Attach them to miniature pumpkins, lady apples, pomegranates, or flower heads.

## Guests of Honor

There are several options for deciding where you and your new hubby will sit at the reception. At a dais, bride and groom are seated in the center of the long, rectangular table overlooking the reception. The best man sits to the bride's right, the maid of honor sits to the groom's left, and the rest of the bridal party all sit on the same side of the table, continuing the alternating male-female pattern. This formal arrangement allows bride and groom to survey all the festivities and gives the guests a clear view of the newlyweds. However, many people do not like this traditional arrangement, finding it uncomfortable or old-fashioned, or preferring that their wedding attendants be seated with their dates.

Sometimes bride and groom choose to be seated with their parents or siblings or at a table with the best man, maid of honor, and their dates. A practical and romantic choice is the sweetheart table, where bride and groom sit alone at a table for two. Newlyweds spend little time sitting during the reception, and this arrangement won't leave a permanent hole at their table but will allow them a few semiprivate moments when they are seated. Another popular choice is for the bride and groom to be seated at one long banquet table, with wedding attendants, their dates, and other close friends seated on both sides of the table. Whichever option you choose, make it prominent and befitting for guests of honor.

- Place them in tiny terra-cotta pots.

- Cut their edges with scalloped scissors.

- Wrap them around napkins, place names at the top of individual menus, or write the names on paper or vellum strips and wrap each around a votive candle or favor.

- Use a gold or silver paint pen to write directly on a leaf.

- Purchase prepackaged cards with an appropriate letterpress motif, and have a calligrapher paint a flower or your new monogram on each card.

Place cards can be printed, written out by hand using good penmanship, or rendered in calligraphy. A nice alternative is a seating chart, which can be a creative collage or piece of artwork, a well-designed chart, or a calligraphed  listing of guests' names and table numbers. You can also forgo place cards altogether by creating an alphabetized list of names with table numbers and ask an usher or maître d' to greet guests and direct them to their table. Your seating arrangements should be given to the reception hall or caterer a few days before the event. Whatever you choose, the guests' names must be arranged alphabetically so that they can find their tables easily.

Table numbers can be equally creative. Calligraphy is very popular for table numbers, and an unembellished, beautifully written card may be all you want. It can be a tented card or a flat card fastened to a beautiful holder, placed in a decorative picture frame or propped up against the centerpiece. Table numbers can be crafted from beads and wire or painted on gilded wood, inscribed on paper and wrapped around pillar candles, or

ABOVE: *Round tables are probably the most popular choice for reception seating. Typically, tables are either 48 or 60 inches (121cm or 152cm) in diameter, providing comfortable seating for, respectively, six to eight people or eight to ten people.*

even embroidered on the sides of the tablecloth or on the napkins. You can use house numbers purchased from a hardware store, numbers on leaded blocks from an antique printing press, or numbers from old road signs.

If you really want to get creative, identify your tables with names. Use the names of places where the two of you have vacationed, love songs, dates that are important to you, love quotes, or pairs of famous lovers. Name each table for a flower, and use that flower as the focus of the centerpiece.

## A Matter of Record

Your wedding is both a life-changing ceremony and a legal rite, and both aspects of the event will be documented in a variety of ways. Both the official paperwork—your marriage license—and the more sentimental records of the day serve to solidify the importance and validity of your marriage, emotionally and legally. A few things to consider:

**Marriage license.** Your legal marriage license needs to be signed by you and your husband, the officiant, and the witnesses. It must be mailed to the state authority within a certain period of time (which differs from state to state), so entrust it to someone dependable, and ask him or her to make a copy of it before putting it in the mail. Once it has been recorded by

*Above: As an alternative to place cards, hire a calligrapher to create a table chart showing guests where they are to sit, and display it in a beautiful setting near the entrance to the reception.*

the government, an official certificate of marriage will be sent to you. While this is a vital document, it is not a beautiful one, and you may wish to have a keepsake of a different sort to commemorate this momentous step.

**Decorative certificate:** Hire an artist, designer, or calligrapher to create a beautiful marriage license that can be framed. In the Jewish faith, the ketubah is a legally binding contract of marriage that is also beautifully rendered for display.

**Guest book:** Ask your guests to compose a special thought in a traditional guest book, which can be made of cloth or petal paper or decorated to suit the season. A fun alternative is to provide an instant camera near the guest book. Guests can photograph themselves, or you can assign the task to someone with a good eye, and photos can instantly be placed in an album with prepasted photo corners next to the guest's signature or comments. There are many interesting alternatives to a standard guest book. Ask guests to sign a plain white platter with ceramic paint pens, which can be baked in a standard oven later for permanency. Provide little note cards and envelopes for guests to write wishes and wisdom to be placed in a beautiful bowl or birdcage. Later, the notes can be placed in an album or bound together into a little booklet. Mat a large engagement photo of the two of you and ask guests to sign the mat. After the wedding, you can exchange the engagement picture for a wedding photo before framing. Create a scroll or guest register with your names and wedding date for guests to sign. Or purchase a coffee table book appropriate for the occasion—such as a book about the location where you are marrying or a book about sunflowers if that is your theme—and have guests write remarks on a page of their choosing.

**Other keepsakes:** Put together a scrapbook of the entire experience, from the moment you got engaged until you return from your honeymoon. Personal wedding vows or readings from your ceremony can be written in calligraphy with your names and the wedding date and framed so that you can look at them every day. Dry your bouquet and your groom's boutonniere to add to a shadow box. Create a family tree showing the grafting of your two lineages.

ABOVE: *The flowing calligraphy on this elegant place card is enhanced by a graceful wheat pattern embossed in gold. Contrasts between the textures of burlap, satin, and lace used on this table create a rich effect.*

## Capturing the Memories

Photography and videography provide the clearest remembrances of the day. When the wedding is over, looking at the recorded images will instantly bring it all back to life. The professionals responsible for these aspects of the wedding will have to work very closely with each other and with you. They'll be following you around all day, recording every action and emotion. Be sure you feel comfortable with both of these people.

Begin searching for your photographer as soon as possible, as they sometimes commit to events far in advance. View samples of finished work, and try to see unedited contact sheets or prints from an entire event so that you can get a sense of how good the outtakes were. Check for pleasing composition, sharp focus, and flattering lighting. Do you feel this person can capture the spirit of the event? Are all the important moments covered? Do the pictures all look the same, or is there interesting variety from shot to shot? Do the people look relaxed and happy? Be clear about your photographic preferences: portraits versus candids, black and white versus color, formal versus photojournalistic—or a combination of all. Make sure you feel confident that this person can deliver what you want, because you won't get a second chance at photographing your wedding day.

Some photography studios can also provide videography or recommend a reliable vendor. As with the photographer, try to review samples of both edited and unedited footage to see how well the videographer captured the day and judge his editing skills. Review the tapes for proper lighting, good sound, important content, and overall style.

As with your other wedding vendors, once you are ready to make a commitment, get it in writing. Your contract will outline exactly what the services and costs are, including the number of hours, quantity and description of tapes or albums (including the number and size of prints), and costs for additional prints. Have the name of the person contracted to do the work listed in the agreement, as large studios sometimes make substitutions if a person is not specified. It is common for the artist to retain the copyright and the negatives or raw footage from your wedding. Some, however, are happy to turn everything over to you after the event, so make sure this is clear in advance and outlined in writing. Be prepared to place a deposit when you sign the contract.

## Snap to It!

The easiest way to infuse your photos with seasonal spirit is to take them outside. Pose for formal portraits in a setting of multihued trees on a nice day in autumn. Take off your shoes and make sure the photographer gets a shot of the green lawn tickling your toes. Ask him to capture the moment you come out of the church into the snowy white winter, or the best man sheltering you both with an enormous umbrella from a sudden summer shower while you greet guests in the receiving line.

Find out if your ceremony and reception sites impose any restrictions regarding photography or videography, and make sure the vendors have the information. Make a shoot list for both professionals of everything and everyone you want photographed. Designate someone other than yourself to be their contact on the wedding day, point out who's who, make sure they've taken all the important shots, or alert them to upcoming events.

ABOVE: *Many people today are opting for a candid, photojournalistic style for their wedding photography. Shot in black and white or in color, these pictures tell the story of the day and are fascinating in and of themselves.*

## Strike Up the Band

Music adds a layer to your wedding that is intangible yet essential to the success of the day. It provides a rich background in the prelude before the ceremony, surrounds you and paces you during processional and recessional, and can interject cherished musical interludes to add dimension to the ceremony itself. In a house of worship, you may have limited options about your choices of music and musicians. You may be restricted to using a church organist or choir or find that only liturgical musical selections are approved. Check with your clergyman for guidelines. In a secular ceremony, your options are wide open. You may choose a string quartet, harpist, or jazz trio, classical guitar, keyboardist, or vocal soloist. Hire a group specifically for the ceremony, use the same band (or a single band member) who will play at the reception, or ask a talented friend or relative to participate in the service. It is even possible to have a disc jockey play recorded music during the ceremony without it seeming obviously "canned."

For the reception, a live band or orchestra is the common choice for formal affairs. Semiformal or informal events may choose between live music and a professional disc jockey. Either way, these seasoned professionals can make or break your event. They are responsible for keeping the pace moving and the party lively. They understand how to take the music down a notch during the meal and to get guests back on their feet between courses. Versatility is ideal. The musical selections should appeal to a cross-section of your guests, not just one age group. Rock and roll can be supplemented with a sampling of salsa, show tunes, disco, and lounge music. With the growing interest in ballroom dancing, incorporating swing, jitterbug, cha-chas, and fox trots will have everyone up on their feet.

A band will usually supply you with a tape of an event for your review to help you decide if you like their style. If possible, try also to see them in action. It's the best way to judge their performance and

## Popular Music Selections

### Processional music:

Voluntary in D (Clarke)

Wedding March (Mozart)

Canon in D (Pachelbel)

Bridal Chorus (Wagner)

The Four Seasons (Vivaldi)

Sleeping Beauty (Tchaikovsky)

Water Music (Handel)

Grow Old Along with Me (Lennon)

Long Ships (Enya)

Hymn (Vangelis)

### Recessional music:

Wedding March (Mendelssohn)

Trumpet Tune in C (Purcell)

Trumpet Tune (Stanley)

Ode to Joy (Beethoven)

Arrival of the Queen of Sheba (Handel)

Benedictus (Simon and Garfunkel)

From This Moment On (Porter)

The Wedding Song (Stookey)

Caribbean Blue (Enya)

Signed, Sealed, Delivered (Wonder)

### First-dance songs:

Someone to Watch Over Me (Gershwin)

It Had to Be You (Jones and Kahn)

Can You Feel the Love Tonight
(John and Rice)

What a Wonderful World
(Douglas and Weiss)

In My Life (Lennon and McCartney)

Unforgettable (Gordon)

### Father-daughter-dance songs:

My Heart Belongs to Daddy (Porter)

Through the Years (Dorff and Panzer)

Butterfly Kisses (Carlisle and Thomas)

My Girl (Robinson and White)

Thank Heaven for Little Girls
(Lerner and Loewe)

What a Wonderful World (Armstrong)

Brown-Eyed Girl (Morrison)

Isn't She Lovely? (Wonder)

Forever Young (Stewart)

Take Good Care of My Baby
(Goffin and King)

see how they handle the crowd. Once you're sold, make sure your contract outlines the names of the performers, what instruments will be played, the hours they will play, how many breaks they'll take and for how long, and what will happen during that time (such as playing a prerecorded tape so there is no dead air). Of course, fees and payment terms should be listed, including costs for overtime.

For the event itself, create a playlist (or even a "don't play" list), give them a copy of the schedule, and make sure they have the names of the major players, such as anyone who has been asked to make a toast. Let them know about any special announcements you wish to make, any cultural dances or traditions they will need music for, and which wedding traditions (announced entrance, garter or bouquet toss, first dance, cake cutting) you will observe. Let them know if music requests from guests are welcome and

# Gâteau Glossary

**buttercream:** made of butter, eggs, and sugar; can be used to frost or fill the cake or for piped decorations

**rolled fondant:** a sugar dough that can be rolled to a thin layer and draped over the cake; creates a smooth, porcelainlike finish

**whipped cream:** heavy cream whipped to stiff peaks, sometimes combined with a stabilizer for more durability; delicious for filling or frosting, but very delicate

**marzipan:** almond-and-sugar dough that can be rolled and draped over a cake, or modeled into shapes of fruit or flowers to be used on the cake or separately

**ganache:** a combination of melted chocolate and cream; can be poured over a cake for an even finish or whipped to filling or frosting consistency

**royal icing:** made of whipped sugar and egg whites; dries to a rock-hard consistency; great for piping scrolls, ropes, and flowers

**pastillage or gum paste:** a sugar dough that is edible but not very tasty; used to model intricate flowers and ribbons; dries to a porcelainlike finish that can be painted with edible food colors

**chocolate modeling dough or chocolate plastic:** melted chocolate and corn syrup kneaded into a malleable dough that can be rolled and draped over a cake like fondant or molded into flowers like pastillage; tasty but difficult to work with

**spun sugar or angel hair:** melted, caramelized sugar 'spun' into fine, golden threads with a cut whisk; very delicate; must be used shortly after it is made

**molded, curled, or ribboned chocolate:** tempered, melted chocolate used to create other shapes; may have transfer patterns applied to its smooth surface

**pulled or blown sugar:** molten sugar modeled into intricate shapes; dries to a glasslike finish; very difficult to master

if anyone who feels moved to do so may give a toast. If there is a song you want played that is not already in their repertoire, be prepared to provide sheet music or, in the case of a disc jockey, a CD with the song you wish to hear.

## The Sweet Life

Your wedding cake is a slice of seasonality waiting to happen. While many still adore a towering white traditional confection, the wedding cake is one place where people often feel free to apply creative license. Classic, elegant, artistic, or downright whimsical, the cake of your dreams is the meal's grand finale and a perfect place to interject personal style.

Often, the caterer will supply a wedding cake for the reception, but if you want something special, you may have to go directly to a baker. Ask your caterer for recommendations to help you find specialty bakers. Usually three or four months before the wedding is enough time to begin your search for this very important cake. Make an appointment to meet, and bring along any designs of which you are particularly fond. If you choose to offer an array of sweets along with wedding cake for the

dessert course, find out if the baker will be able to provide the other pastries also. Taste tests are very important—whether your cake is the only dessert to be served or will be accompanied by other dessert courses, it must taste as good as it looks. And its looks must last since it will be on display during the reception. Be sure to let the baker know if you're planning an outdoor event during the summer so that preparations can be taken to make sure the cake can take the heat.

When it comes to flavor, anything goes these days—devil's food cake with white chocolate hazelnut ganache, carrot and ginger cake with orange buttercream, marble cheesecake covered in fondant, or almond cake with raspberry conserve, to name just a few. Color can be applied as liberally as you dare, allowing an easy way to link your cake to your color palette. Decorate your cake with fresh flowers, press edible petals into the sides of the tiers, use gilded nuts and berries on each layer, create a cascade of chocolate seashells, or add pastillage butterflies to a garden of sugar flowers. Pipe royal icing snowflakes on the sides, or mound the top of each tier with piles of coconut "snow." Stencil a daisy pattern on the frosting, or quilt the fondant covering to match the table-cloth. Cakes may be priced by the slice or by the size of the tiers, and you can bet that the more embellishments you want, the more expensive it will be.

Some decorative cakes are designed with some sort of finishing touch on the top tier, but if you still need to top the cake, use your parents' vintage bride-and-groom cake topper, fill a small compote dish with sugared flowers or small fruits, have a three-dimensional monogram made to stand on top, or have a topper made to order that looks like you and your groom. Place your bouquet on top of the cake, or have a duplicate made expressly for your topper. Fabric or pulled-sugar ribbons or bows cascading down the sides create a dramatic look. A bird's nest can be spun of golden angel hair and filled with blown-sugar eggs. Plan to display your cake throughout the reception; this work of art should be admired. Make sure the size of the table is proportionate to the cake. A beautiful cake table can be simply covered with a beautiful cloth and propped with a cake knife, plate and forks, and two champagne glasses. Or tie it to the season by adding fall leaves, gilded pine-cones, seashells, Christmas ornaments, a birdhouse, ivy, or of course flowers.

OPPOSITE: *This innovative couple chose to build an edible centerpiece for their guests. Terms of endearment—used instead of table numbers at this event—are piped in gold onto plaques adorning each table's cake. Surrounded by plump roses, the cake invites guests to savor its beauty until the end of the evening, when the catering staff will serve it at each table.*

# Happy Holidays

## Summer

The whole season feels like one big holiday, but if you want your guests to have stars in their eyes—stars and stripes, that is—Independence Day is the money ticket in July. While the day may not seem very wedding-y, many patriotic American couples enjoy including a few elements in their July wedding that recognize the holiday. Serve a white cake with red raspberries and blueberries piled on its tiers and filled with alternating layers of raspberry preserves, white chocolate buttercream, and blueberry conserve. Give sparklers as favors. Have the wedding near a location that has fireworks, and time your "I dos" to coincide with the beginning of the show. Have your bridesmaids carry bouquets of red tulips and blue hydrangeas. Add white roses or peonies to yours. Ask the men to wear navy suits, white shirts, and red ties. If you choose to display the flag somewhere, treat it with the respect it deserves.

## Autumn

If Halloween is your favorite holiday, you'll have a hard time giving up on the idea of using its many motifs somewhere in your wedding. And there's no reason that you shouldn't use them! With a modicum of good taste, this holiday wedding can be celebrated with as much elegance or whimsy as you like. Decorate masks, add table-seating information to them, and use them in lieu of place cards. Give each guest a goody bag with candy corn and an inexpensive magic trick for a favor. Have an elegant costume ball right out of *Romeo and Juliet* (only with a happy ending). If you're feeling particularly playful, play spooky music during the cocktail hour, and have the bar set up with containers of dry ice (out of the reach of guests) emitting creepy fog. Carve a pumpkin with a beautiful pattern and use it as a floral container for the centerpiece. If Thanksgiving is more to your liking, serve a traditional turkey dinner and create a jewellike cranberry wreath for each table to encircle an arrangement of Indian corn and pillar candles. Give pumpkin-scented candles as favors. Instead of (or in addition to!) wedding cake, serve every type of pie you can think of for dessert. Don't forget to make a speech of thanks to all your guests.

BELOW: *Guest favors are a great spot to introduce a theme or develop a color palette. Here, the colors of autumn are brought indoors for this forest of favors.*

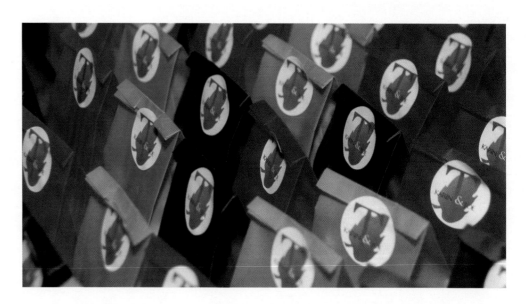

ABOVE: *A signature dessert can be used to highlight the holiday. This heart-felt Valentine could either accompany or substitute for the wedding cake.*

## Winter

This season is chock-full of holidays, each rich in symbolism and festivity. For your Christmas wedding, use miniature live evergreen trees decorated with tiny ornaments as your centerpieces. Afterward, let one guest at each table take home a tree, or plant them someplace special for your very own nuptial forest. Write your guests' names and table numbers on iridescent glass Christmas balls and hang them on a tree near the reception entrance. Have your wedding cake made to look like a stack of Christmas presents. Kwanzaa is a holiday based on seven principles of traditional African values, important doctrine to remember at such a significant event. List the Nguzo Saba (the Seven Principles) in Swahili and English in your wedding program. Decorate with brilliant African prints, African art objects, baskets, and fruits and vegetables. Display the Kinara (seven-stemmed candle-holder) in a prominent place, or use it as a centerpiece on each table.

Gifts—in this case, favors—should have an artistic or educational nature; small books would be ideal. For New Year's Eve, have a black and white wedding with a midnight candlelight ceremony, give each guest a split of champagne, or dress to the hilt in metallics, sequins, or beads. To honor the Chinese New Year, infuse the wedding with lucky red and the symbol of the new year, serve a traditional banquet meal on lazy Susans, or perform the tea ceremony. Use red and pink as your palette on Valentine's Day for everything from programs to place cards, clothing to cake. Let the heart icon pervade on invitations, napkin rings, and even food.

## Spring

Another flurry of holidays brings a season's worth of ideas. Show your Irish spirit on St. Patrick's Day by using a Celtic motif on your stationery items—invitations, programs, place cards, and thank-you notes. Hire a bagpiper to play at the wedding ceremony or during the cocktail hour. Create a floral centerpiece in the shape of a four-leaf clover. For the jesters among you, try to hold back on April Fools' Day. Consider using a harlequin pattern on your tablecloths, such as a white-on-white jacquard or ivory and gold print, and repeat the pattern on the sides of your cake. Copy the jesters from a deck of cards onto your place cards and table numbers. The parade of holidays in spring can inspire you to have your own—an Easter parade, that is. Plan a leisurely stroll with your guests through the streets from ceremony to reception, and remind the women to wear hats (yourself included). Use empty, clean eggshells set in a delicate eggcups to hold small flowers or tea lights at each place setting. Give decorative marble or enameled eggs as your favors, or make tiny Easter baskets for each guest—and don't forget to include lilies as a floral focal point. When May Day rolls around, use the flowing ribbons of the maypole as beautiful backdrops at your outdoor ceremony.

## Deck the Halls

If your wedding date coincides with a holiday, you might choose to incorporate some of the themes of the festival to your advantage. Some holidays, such as Christmas, lend themselves to color choices and decorating schemes, while others, such as April Fools' Day, could easily turn tasteless if not handled with sophistication. By using subtlety in your effects, you allow the influences of the holiday to inspire your wedding style without overshadowing it. Depending on the holiday, you may find ways to shape your palette, stationery items, menu, music, decorations, favors, or clothing to suit the occasion. Judging how much is too much is a matter of taste, but if in doubt, leave it out.

## Gifts of Love

At one time, giving small gifts to your wedding guests as a gesture of thanks was a cultural or regional matter. Nowadays, the custom has become quite popular, and creative and interesting ideas abound. Favors need not be costly or large; in fact, it is preferable if they are not, as they are sometimes left behind. A food item or useful handcrafted article may be appreciated more than something that seems like a souvenir of your wedding.

Favors may be placed at each table setting, handed out personally by the bride and groom, or arranged near the door and taken as people leave the reception. It is a way to thank guests for joining you and show how much you appreciated their company. Favors are not necessary and sometimes not even expected, so if your budget is stretched pretty thin, this can be the first thing to eliminate.

Food is always an appropriate and appreciated gift. Brew up a batch of homemade wedding ale and bottle it with your own personal label. Slices of groom's cake in handsome boxes, chocolates (truffles or filled candies in shapes to conform to your wedding style), decorated cookies, and Jordan almonds wrapped in tulle are common. Miniature jars of homemade jam, aromatic tea bags wrapped with a honey stick in a garage-sale china teacup, small bottles of sake, or a small treasure chest filled with gold-wrapped chocolate coins for a beach wedding would be charming. Small bottles of maple syrup are perfect at an autumn wedding in New England, as are packages of hot chocolate in

---

### Favor Ideas

- dried flower topiaries in miniature terra-cotta pots

- a pair of beeswax taper candles, held together with a band inscribed with your monogram

- a beautiful Christmas ornament

- an origami heart

- seed packets, flowering bulbs, or tree saplings

- handmade soap

- beautiful shells

- a handheld, battery-operated mini fan

the cold of winter. A miniature bird's nest filled with chocolate eggs seems right for spring, and a wrapped candy apple is a nice treat for your late-fall wedding.

Choosing favors with that can perform double duty makes a lot of sense. Create a compact disc with favorite love songs or music from your wedding, and print a cover for the case of each CD with your names and wedding date, as well as the name and table number of the guest, so that the disk can double as the place card. Other clever combinations: use miniature picture frames to hold each place card; use votive holders on your reception tables to provide illumination and give each guest a spare votive candle with a note encouraging them to take home a holder; or make breakaway centerpieces with enough bud vases or small potted plants that each guest can take one home at the end of the day.

*Above: Wrapped to perfection and placed at each setting, favors will finish dressing the tables. Coordinate the colors of the wrapping with the colors used on the table and in the centerpieces.*

When it comes to gift giving, don't forget the people who have been your support system through all of this—the wedding party. Gifts for your attendants don't have to be expensive but should be well thought out to show your sincere appreciation for their friendship and help. If you're a do-it-yourselfer, feel free to make something for your friends as the ultimate personal expression of thanks—a pampering basket of bath oils, body scrubs, mud masks, and herbal elixirs; a pair of inlaid wood bookends; or a personal scrapbook of the friendship you have shared. When purchasing gifts for your attendants, choose something that would be appropriate for any occasion and that you think the person will really enjoy and use. Gifts for the bridesmaids and groomsmen can be essentially similar, or each can be handpicked but of equal value. Earrings, tie tacks, perfume bottles, jewelry boxes, handmade cases for business cards, a fine pen or lighter, a beautiful scarf, a gift certificate, or a new golf club will be welcome.

As a general rule, people tend to prefer items that are not inscribed with someone else's name. Your attendants may appreciate a silver compact engraved with their own name rather than yours and your groom's. For ultrapersonaliza-tion, have the gift engraved with a personal message from you to your friend. Hand the gifts out at the rehearsal dinner or any-time during the week before the wedding, and include a short note of thanks.

## Exit: Stage Left

How will you get around on your wedding day? Choose a method that fits your style and budget, whether that means renting a fleet of stretch limos for the entire wedding party or hopping in your brother's Humvee. Rolls Royces, classic cars, and vintage convertibles are available for livery rental, and each will certainly introduce its own variety of style. While changing into a swimsuit and exiting on water skis may be a bit over the top, step-ping onto a waiting sailboat or gondola after your waterside wedding and sailing off into the sunset is the epitome of romance. Couples have been known to enter or exit on horse-back, by hot-air balloon, by horse and carriage, and by motorcycle. However you go, make sure someone else is responsible for driving that day. You and your groom will have enough on your plates without having to worry about driving to and from the wedding.

When hiring a vehicle to chauffeur you for the day, find out if the costs are based on an hourly charge or a day rate and if taxes and tips are included. There may be a minimum number of hours required, and you will surely have to place a deposit. Be clear about the payment terms for the balance; if the remainder of the fee has to be paid on the day of your wedding, consider assigning the responsibility to one of the attendants. Check to be sure that insurance and licenses are in order, as well as the cars themselves, and ask for references. Discuss the driver's attire for the day, and make sure he has the directions ahead of time. If the vehicle is hired to bring you to the ceremony and reception only, arrange in advance with someone from the wedding party to take the two of you home. And when it's all over, relax, kiss your honey, open gifts, write thank-yous, go for a pedicure, kiss your honey again, and enjoy being a newlywed. Above all, season's greetings, whatever the time of year.

ABOVE: *Shout it at the top of your lungs! Write it in the sky in puffs of smoke. On this day, you'll want to share your joy with the entire world. Make sure everyone knows that you're "Just Married."*

Spring is in the air, and the whole world is lighter. There's a flurry of activity as Mother Nature begins her handiwork again, casting off the doldrums of winter. When you see the first buds of green appearing on the trees and the first crocus or daffodil poking through the soil, your heart soars. You can't help but smile. Butterflies and bumblebees and ladybugs make their appearance, busy with their spring labors. The sound of birds chirping wakes you every morning, but you don't mind a bit. This is the rebirth: a time for reinventing oneself, for starting something new…a perfect time for a wedding.

Let the lighthearted nature of the season shine throughout your special day. Airy fabrics, cheery colors, and amusing elements will all put bounce in your nuptials. Use the tender offerings of the season's first produce when planning your menu. Throw in a solid dose of cheerful optimism— certainly no problem on your wedding day—for a spirited spring fling.

## Tea for Two (Plus 150)

After a formal morning ceremony, the newlyweds and their attendants are whisked away for a flurry of photographs, leaving guests to fend for themselves until the appropriate hour for tea. Information on local attractions, such as the botanical gardens, museums, and quaint shops, are outlined in the back of the wedding program. Also included are the names, addresses, and telephone numbers of several gracious friends of the family who have offered to open their homes to anyone in need. With each choice will come a different experience this day. You opt for the latter, and choose well. Your charming host offers light refreshments, and you know you have to hold back because the day is just beginning. Several hours and many delightful conversations later, it is time to reconvene at the hotel.

It is a grand old dame of a hotel, built in a previous era and still in pristine condition. This Victorian beauty holds all of her original charisma; the surroundings instantly transport you back in time. You love this place. You've been here before for afternoon tea and know exactly where to go

ABOVE: *Baskets of petals stand ready for guests to grab by the handful, and will make a festive send-off for the bride and groom after the ceremony.*

OPPOSITE: *Peonies, tulips, ranunculus, and roses make up this bountiful bouquet of spring blossoms in shades of pink and white.*

when you enter the lobby. On this special day, the tea salon is closed to the public, and the room has been decorated specifically for the wedding. It is a charming, buoyant place, overlooking the gardens, which are magnificent on this bright, sunny day in April. Beds of daffodils and tulips overlap as one fades and the other thrives. Full-grown hyacinth and miniature muscari dot the stone path. Cherry blossom and dogwood trees will provide shade for the weathered stone benches below when their burgeoning buds burst into a floral riot.

Inside, the standard short tea tables have been replaced with round dinner tables in several sizes. Some are set for a party of four, some for six, but none more than eight, to retain the feeling of intimacy while taking tea. Tables are already set with teacups and accoutrements, with a droll floral teapot placed in the center. Don't be concerned about your tea getting cold—this teapot is the centerpiece, and stems of spring blooms jut out from its lid. Today's repast will be served buffet style, but tea will be served at the tables. A gloved waiter appears when you've settled into your seat to find out your preference for tea and offers a glass of champagne or sherry. You choose sherry and China oolong, then turn to survey the room. The harpist, in her usual spot near the dance floor, starts the music at a quiet pace. Later she will be joined by a pianist and strings in case anyone wants to show off their ballroom dancing skills. There is a picturesque assortment of hats on the female guests, befitting a proper tea. A bit of a stir sweeps the room and all eyes turn toward the entrance as the bride and groom enter unannounced. They look radiant. Her draped, beaded gown looks like it was made to be worn in this room.

The buffet table is beautifully arranged with levels of tea trays cradling a tempting assortment of traditional and nontraditional fare and decorated with antique cups and saucers filled with flowers. You start with the traditional: scones—done in miniature— with clotted cream and blackberry preserves, although the rosemary jelly is very tempting. A selection of tea sandwiches is a must. Cucumber, watercress, egg mayonnaise, shrimp salad, and curried chicken are all accounted for, and so are smoked salmon, cream cheese and chives, thinly sliced ham with apricot jam, and triangular Neapolitans filled with tomato and asparagus. Creamy quiches are sliced and beckoning, and grilled

OPPOSITE: *A sea of petals carpets the aisle at this outdoor ceremony. At the altar, an arch covered in tulle and adorned with generous spring blooms frames the couple as they listen closely to the words of the officiant.*

ABOVE: *This lighthearted table is set for a wedding tea, a popular alternative to the sit-down dinner reception. Spring flowers burst forth from a wire-work teapot lined with sheet moss. Each guest will take home the miniature flower arrangement in the matching teacup at every place setting.*

ABOVE: *Miniature tiered cakes are sized for
individual portions. These petite pastries can
be served in lieu of a slice of wedding cake,
or boxed up for your guests to bring home
as an edible favor.*

chicken breasts, marinated in lemon and thyme and served with fresh biscuits and tender asparagus, are offered for anyone who wishes something more substantial. There are more choices than you have room for, and you're saving yourself for dessert. Back at your table, you carefully pour the milk into your cup before pouring the tea. A passing waiter gives you an approving nod. Clearly you know how this is done.

The music is in full swing and the newlyweds are sweeping around the dance floor in an elegant waltz. Waiters circulate regularly, freshening teapots and tidbits, keeping everything tidy. For dessert, there are strawberry shortcakes, slices of lemon poppy seed cakes, rhubarb and rose petal tarts, tea ice cream, wedges of Granny Smith apples spread with Stilton, and a traditional assortment of miniature pastries.

The wedding cake seems almost secondary, though its porcelain finish is a perfect reproduction of the pattern on the flower-filled teacup resting on the top tier, and you can't help but wonder what enchantment awaits beneath its iced exterior. The cake table is dressed simply with scattered rose petals and the bride's bouquet, set into a teapot of the same pattern as the cake topper. Bride and groom cut the cake with an antique set, serving each other tenderly. Moments later, they lift their glasses in a touching round of toasts: to their parents, their attendants, and all their guests, expressing the joy that they feel. When the guests begin to take their leave, the newlyweds station themselves near the door, handing each woman a flower-filled teacup and saucer. For the men, there are cigars to enjoy later. For the guests and the happy couple alike, there is a memory of a bright spring wedding that suited all to a "tea."

## The Picnic in the Park

Shuttle service is provided into the park from a nearby parking garage the couple has rented for the day, and traveling in groups gets the guests in the spirit of fun from the start. The landmark picnic house which is closed to normal traffic, sits in the center of the park, surrounded by shady trees and rolling meadows. The ceremony takes place on the patio, only partially secluded from the public by flowering hedges and trees. Rows of white wooden folding chairs are decorated with sprigs of lilac, and the tall supporting columns of the building are draped with garlands of flowers and greens. The music is modern and ethereal, and when everyone seems to be seated, the procession begins.

Only the bride and groom are formally dressed: she in a bouncy ball gown of embroidered organza, he in an ivory dinner jacket with one perfect rose in his lapel. Attendants were asked to choose their own garments…men in black suits with a lavender tie purchased for them, women in an outfit of any sort as long as it was solid lavender on the bottom and solid black on the top, or vice versa. The attendants made wonderful choices: a mini halter dress with a black satin empire bodice and a lavender crepe skirt, black chiffon palazzo pants with a lavender sweater set, a long A-line organza skirt in lavender with a black silk tank top, a short sleeveless black sheath with a lavender bolero jacket. The flower girl and ring bearer, also a girl, are both dressed in lavender party dresses, one with a black sash that gathers into a bow in the back, the other with a sparse pattern of delicate black flowers embroidered on her bodice. When they are all together, each is perfectly coordinated with the rest, yet the overall look is unique and interesting.

After the ceremony, the young couple exit the patio and stand under a shady tree with their parents, greeting their guests and gathering good wishes. The catering staff deftly whisks away the chairs to be placed inside at the dinner tables and sets up a light repast on the patio for guests to nibble on while the wedding party poses for formal photographs nearby. At the bar, there is lemonade, punch, iced tea, wine, beer, and champagne from which to choose. The table has been draped with garlands to match those on the columns—a lovely effect. The hour passes swiftly, and people wander into the historic building to look around.

ABOVE: *A pastel palette is perfect for spring. Bountiful sweet peas burst from a napkin and add color and texture to the plate, while a pattern of dragonflies flits across the table on the organza overlay.*

ABOVE: *Intimate tables require decoration on a small scale, in contrast with the breathtaking expanse of scenery.*

OPPOSITE: *In this table setting a sheer checked cloth is hand painted with butterflies. Ersatz dragonflies are tucked into the centerpiece and repeated elegantly in the golden napkin ring.*

# Springtime Specialties

- Perky polka dots add retro charm to anything they touch.

- Outfit your maids with stylish purses covered with flowers instead of bouquets.

- Create a maypole with cascading trails of ribbon blowing in the balmy breeze.

- Cover your bouquet with tulle for an ethereal look.

- For favors, give your guests tree seedlings to plant.

- Use petal paper for your invitations, or emboss them with a tree motif.

- Place a small guest book at each table and create a library of fond wishes.

- Adorn place cards with fresh flowers. A stem of lily of the valley or muscari is just the right size.

- Illuminate the outdoors with paper luminaries.

- A basket weave is the perfect embellishment for your wedding cake. Use berries and other small fruits to decorate it instead of flowers.

- Build folding screens out of picket fencing and hang with pots of flowering plants.

- Use flowering herbs or nontoxic flowers with thick, long stems as swizzle sticks for your drinks.

- Have each of your attendants carry a bouquet of a different pastel color.

- Marry in a garden and surround yourself with spring.

- Use watering cans as the containers for your centerpieces.

- Pastel colors are a natural in spring.

- Change into white capri pants and make your getaway on a bicycle built for two.

- Add special touches to your flowers, such as artificial butterflies in the arrangements or an antique lace handkerchief to wrap around the stems of your bouquet.

The building, inset on a hill in the park, is actually two stories. Level with the grounds at the patio entrance, the back of the room is one flight up from the inclined park. Glass doors open onto another stone patio that overlooks the green meadow below. At the entrance, a tabletop is completely covered with grass, and rows of lavender-colored tulips in water tubes have been inserted into the grass. Each has a single paper leaf attached, on which the seating assignments are written.

Salads have already been plated and set at each seat, and they are dotted with colorful edible flowers. The tables are covered in floor-length lavender cloths, with an organza overlay in a large checked pattern. It is starting to get dark, and waiters begin to light the candles on the tables. Flowers are abundant throughout the room, and the effect is of an upscale picnic. Food will be served family-style tonight, with large platters set on each table and everyone helping themselves. One of the bride's close friends, a professional dancer, has composed a short piece to present at the reception, and for a few minutes, everyone is transfixed by her performance.

As darkness sets in outside, the tables begin to glow from within. Each has been outfitted underneath with a battery-operated lantern to illuminate the tablecloth. The band keeps the pace going throughout the evening, pumping it up between courses to keep the crowd on their feet.

Dessert tonight is appropriately picniclike. The groom's aunts and cousins have each contributed a specialty cookie. The sumptuous cookie buffet is styled on levels by the caterer. Instead of cake, there is a cupcake display. Platters of frosted cupcakes, decorated with delicate sugar flowers, are set on a tiered tabletop plant stand. The cupcake table is decorated with a lavender birdhouse overflowing with flowers, sparkling votives, and two crystal glasses filled with champagne. Cupcakes are served with delightful miniature fruits made of ice cream and sorbets, and waiters pour coffee and tea from silver pots. Dancing continues long into the night, until at last the arrival of the fleet of shuttles signals the end of the evening and guests are transported back to their cars. Tonight, bride and groom will spend their first evening as husband and wife in a bed-and-breakfast town house directly across from the park and dream about their family picnic.

OPPOSITE: *A bicycle built for two may not be a practical getaway vehicle for a bride dressed to the nines, but surely makes for a fun photo. After a quick change into a pair of white bike shorts, you'll be ready to ride off into the sunset.*

# Featured Resources

## Calligraphy

Angela. R. Welch
Pen and Pauper
Orange Beach, AL
(334) 981-1377
penandpauper@hotmail.com
www.angelarwelch.com

Hilary Williams
Hil-Ink Calligraphy
North Hollywood, CA
(818) 760-3406
hilary@hil-ink.com
www.hil-ink.com

Stephannie Barba
Stephannie Barba Calligraphy
San Francisco, CA
(415) 437-6001
stephanniebarba@hotmail.com

Susan L. Ramsey
Calligraphic Creations
Norwalk, CT
(203) 847-5715
calligraphic@aol.com
www.callig.com

## Event Location

The Boathouse in Central Park
Donna Scaramucci
East 72nd Street and Park Drive North
New York, NY 10021
(212) 517-2233

## Event Style

Bette Matthews
Brooklyn, NY
(718) 857-4699
bettematthews@aol.com

## Fashion

Alfred Angelo
116 Welsh Road
Horsham, PA 19044
(866) 226-4356
www.alfredangelo.com

Amsale
347 West 39th Street, Suite 11N
New York, NY 10018
(212) 971-0170

Anne Barge Collection
84 Peachtree Street, Suite 301
Atlanta, GA 30303
(404) 230-9995
www.annebarge.com

Carolina Herrera Ltd.
48 West 38th Street, 3rd floor
New York, NY 10018
(212) 944-5757
www.carolinaherrerabridal.com

Christos Inc.
241 West 37th Street
New York, NY 10018
(212) 921-0025
www.christosbridal.com

Clea Colet
960 Madison Avenue, 2nd floor
New York, NY 10021
(212) 396-4608

Cynthia C. & Co.
414 West Broadway
New York, NY 10012
(212) 966-2200

Galina
260 West 39th Street
New York, NY 10018
(212) 564-1020
www.galinabridal.com

Givenchy
116 Welsh Road
Horsham, PA 19044
(215) 659-5300
www.givenchy.com

Janell Berte Ltd.
248 East Libery Street
Lancaster, PA 17602
(717) 291-9894

Jessica McClintock Inc.
1400 16th Street
San Francisco, CA 94103
(800) 711-8718
www.jessicamcclintock.com

Josephine Sasso
226 East 78th Street
New York, NY 10021
(212) 396-9692

Kirstie Kelly
1265 Seventh Avenue
San Francisco, CA 94122
(415) 665-9685

L'Ezu Atalier
860 South Los Angeles Street, Suite 930
Los Angeles, CA 90014
(213) 622-2422
www.lezu.com

Manale
260 West 39th Street, 11th floor
New York, NY 10001
(212) 944-6939
www.manale.com

Melissa Sweet
70 Rossford Avenue
Fort Thomas, KY 41075
(859) 572-9162
www.melissasweet.com

Paris Tiaras
305 W. Benson Street
Cincinatti, OH 45215
(513) 948-8888

Pat Kerr
200 Wagner Place
Memphis, TN 38103
(901) 525-5223

Priscilla of Boston
40 Cambridge Street
Charlestown, MA 02129
(617) 242-2677
www.priscillaofboston.com

Reem Acra
245 Seventh Avenue, Suite 6B
New York, NY 10001
(212) 414-0980

Tomasina
615 Washington Road
Pittsburgh, PA 15228
(412) 563-7788
www.tomasina.com

Wearkstatt
33 Green Street
New York, NY 10018
(212) 279-3929
www.wearkstatt.com

## Fine Jewelry and Hand-crafted Gifts

The Clay Pot
162 Seventh Avenue
Brooklyn, NY 11215
(718) 788-6564
www.clay-pot.com

## Floral Design

Avi Adler
87 Luquer Street
Brooklyn, NY 11231
(718) 243-0804

Castle & Pierpont
401 East 76th Street
New York, NY 10021
(212) 570-1284

Elizabeth Ryan
411 East Ninth Street
New York, NY 10009
(212) 995-1111
erfloral@aol.com

J. Gordon Designs
146 West 29th Street, 6E
New York, NY 10001
(212) 563-1138

Lisa Marie McWilliams
8 Newbury Lane
Southhampton, NY 11968
(631) 283-4764

Magnolia
Jennifer Pfeiffer
434 Hudson Street
New York, NY
(212) 243-7302

Renny Designs for Entertaining
505 Park Avenue
New York, NY 10022
(212) 288-7000

SBK Associates, Floral Decorators
3 East 63rd Street, Suite #1C
New York, NY 10021
(212) 813-0251

Susan Holland & Company,
Event Design and Catering
142 Fifth Avenue, 4th floor
New York, NY 10011
(212) 807-8892

Tapestry, Bridal & Special Event Flowers
842 Rhode Island Street
San Francisco, CA 94107
(415) 550-1015

Two Design Group
1937 Irving Boulevard, Suite A
Dallas, TX 75207
(214) 741-3145
www.tdgevents.com

Verdure
3014 Benvenue Avenue
Berkeley, CA 94705
(510) 548-7764

*Food*
Ana Paz Cakes
1460 NW 107th Avenue
Miami, FL 33172
(305) 471-5850
www.anapazcakes.com

The Boathouse in Central Park
(*see* Event Location)

Callahan Catering
205 East 95th Street, Suite 10D
New York, NY 10028
(212) 327-1144

Polly's Cakes
Polly Schoonmaker
Portland, OR
(503) 230-1986
www.pollyscakes.com

*Party Rentals*
The Cloth Connection
Michael Davis
by appointment only
80 Red Schoolhouse Road, Suite 215
Spring Valley, NY 10977
(845) 426-3500
www.clothconnection.com

Just Linens
by appointment only
770 Lexington Avenue
New York, NY 10021
(212) 688-8808
www.justlinens.com

TriServe Party Rentals
by appointment only
770 Lexington Avenue
New York, NY 10021
(212) 752-7661

*Photography*
Paul Barnett
4053 Adams Avenue
San Diego, CA 92116
(619) 285-1207
www.barnettphoto.com

Joshua Ets-Hokin
2014 Oakdale Avenue
San Francisco, CA 94124
(415) 255-8645
www.etshokin.com

Karen Hill
86 North 6th Street #205
Brooklyn, NY 11211
(212) 414-5115
www.karenhill.com

Eliot Hotlzman
50 C Street
San Rafael, CA 94901
(415) 457-3980
www.eliotholtzman.com

Lyn Hughes
114 West 27th Street, 6th floor
New York, NY 10001
(212) 645-8417

Martin Jacobs
10 West 15th Street, Suite 1102
New York, NY 10011
(212) 206-0941

Kit Latham
4 Castle Street, #3
Great Barrington, MA 01230
(413) 528-9072
www.kitlatham.com

Roy Llera
9713 N.E. Second Avenue
Miami Shores, FL 33138
(305) 759-2600

Sarah Merians
104 Fifth Avenue, 4th floor
New York, NY 10011
(212) 633-0502

Nancy Palubniak
247 West 35th Street, 10th floor
New York, NY 10001
(212) 629-0142

Antonio Rosario
1 Plaza Street West
Brooklyn, NY 11217
(718) 783-1587
antonio@antoniomrosario.com
www.antoniomrosario.com

Andrea Sperling
102 East 22nd Street, #6H
New York, NY 10010
(212) 674-5314

Tanya Tribble
103 Sullivan Street, Suite D
New York, NY 10012
(212) 431-8066

Therese Marie Wagner
89 Pinckney Road
Red Bank, NJ 07701
(732) 345-0515

Jason Walz
143 South 8th Street
2nd Floor, Apt 2C
Brooklyn, NY 11211
(718) 388-8102

# Index

# Photography and Design Credits

*Page 1:* ©Andrea Sperling

*Page 2:* ©Jason Walz

*Page 5:* ©Andrea Sperling

*Page 7:* ©Lyn Hughes

*Page 8:* ©Sarah Merians

*Page 9:* ©Karen Hill

*Page 10:* ©Andrea Sperling

*Page 11:* ©Karen Hill

*Page 13:* ©Jason Walz

*Page 14:* ©Antonio M. Rosario (food preparation: Peter Callahan and Beth Parker, Executive Chef for Callahan Catering)

*Page 15:* ©Antonio M. Rosario (floral design: Bette Matthews)

*Page 16:* ©Lyn Hughes

*Page 17:* ©Karen Hill

*Page 18:* ©Joshua Ets-Hokin

*Page 19:* ©Antonio M. Rosario (floral design: Lisa Marie McWilliams; linens courtesy of the Cloth Connection; photographed at The Boathouse in Central Park)

*Pages 20-21:* ©Karen Hill

*Page 23:* ©Therese Marie Wagner (tent from Paul David Partyware)

*Page 24:* ©Andrea Sperling

*Page 25:* ©Kit Latham

*Page 27:* ©Kit Latham

*Pages 28-29:* ©Karen Hill (photographed at New York Botanical Garden)

*Page 28:* bottom left ©Antonio M. Rosario (flatware courtesy of TriServe Party Rentals; linens courtesy of Just Linens)

*Page 30:* ©Lyn Hughes

*Page 31:* ©Antonio M. Rosario (food preparation: Peter Callahan and Beth Parker, Executive Chef for Callahan Catering; serving pieces from Callahan Catering)

*Page 32, left:* ©Antonio M. Rosario (linens courtesy of Just Linens; napkin rings from private collection)

*Pages 32-33:* ©Karen Hill (floral design: Susan Holland & Company, Event Design and Catering)

*Page 34:* ©Antonio M. Rosario (calligraphy and invitation design: Stephannie Barba; boutonniere: Elizabeth Ryan; linens courtesy of Just Linens)

*Page 35:* ©Lyn Hughes

*Page 36:* ©Lyn Hughes

*Page 37:* ©Antonio M. Rosario (jewelry courtesy of The Clay Pot; designers from left to right: Barbara Heinrich, Richard Landi, Elizabeth Ryle, Barbara Heinrich, Barbara Heinrich, Richard Landi, Barbara Heinrich, Richard Landi)

*Page 38:* ©Lyn Hughes

*Page 39:* ©Lyn Hughes

*Page 40:* ©Antonio M. Rosario (calligraphy: Stephannie Barba; dishes and tableware courtesy of TriServe Party Rentals; linens courtesy of Just Linens)

*Page 41:* ©Joshua Ets-Hokin

*Page 42:* ©Joshua Ets-Hokin

*Page 43:* ©Jason Walz

*Page 44:* Bridal gown by Priscilla of Boston

*Page 45:* ©Karen Hill

*Page 46:* ©Joshua Ets-Hokin

*Page 48:* ©Andrea Sperling

*Page 49:* ©Therese Marie Wagner (floral design: Jerry Rose Florist)

*Page 50:* ©Antonio M. Rosario (floral design: Elizabeth Ryan; chairs, tables, dishes, and tableware courtesy of TriServe Party Rentals; linens and chair sash courtesy of Just Linens)

*Page 51:* ©Antonio M. Rosario (floral design: Elizabeth Ryan; calligraphy: Stephannie Barba; chairs, tables, dishes, napkin rings, votives, and tableware courtesy of TriServe Party Rentals; linens and chair covers courtesy of Just Linens)

*Page 53:* ©Andrea Sperling

*Page 54:* ©Antonio M. Rosario (floral design: Elizabeth Ryan; dishes and tableware courtesy of TriServe Party Rentals; linens courtesy of Just Linens)

*Page 55:* ©Paul Barnett

*Page 56:* ©Jason Walz

*Page 57:* ©Jason Walz

*Page 58:* ©Lyn Hughes

*Page 59:* ©Joshua Ets-Hokin

*Page 60:* ©Lyn Hughes

*Page 61:* ©Therese Marie Wagner

*Page 62:* ©Matt Savins (floral design: Two Design Group Events)

*Page 63:* ©Kit Latham

*Page 64:* ©Antonio M. Rosario (salt and pepper shakers and silver charger courtesy of TriServe Party Rentals)

*Page 65:* ©Antonio M. Rosario (floral design: Elizabeth Ryan; calligraphy: Bette Matthews; chairs, tables, dishes, and tableware courtesy of TriServe Party Rentals; linens courtesy of Just Linens)

*Page 66:* ©Jason Walz

*Page 67:* ©Therese Marie Wagner (photographed at Tavern on the Green)

*Page 68:* ©Andrea Sperling

*Page 69:* ©Antonio M. Rosario (floral design: Jennifer Pfeiffer/Magnolia; calligraphy: Angela R. Welch/Pen and Pauper; linens courtesy of the Cloth Connection; photographed at The Boathouse in Central Park)

*Page 70:* ©Jason Walz

*Page 71:* ©Andrea Sperling

*Page 72:* ©Antonio M. Rosario (food preparation: Alan Ashkenaze, executive chef for The Boathouse in Central Park; serving tray courtesy of TriServe Party Rentals; photographed at The Boathouse in Central Park)

*Page 73:* ©Antonio M. Rosario (floral design: Bette Matthews; tableware and linens from private collection)

*Page 74:* ©Lyn Hughes

*Page 75:* ©Lyn Hughes

*Page 76:* ©Antonio M. Rosario (food preparation: Peter Callahan and Beth Parker, Executive Chef for Callahan Catering; serving pieces from Callahan Catering)

*Page 77:* ©Therese Marie Wagner

*Page 78:* Cufflinks by Tiffany and Company

*Page 79:* ©Eliot Holtzman

*Page 80:* ©Jason Walz

*Page 81:* Bridal gown by Alfred Angelo

*Page 83:* Bridal gown by Givenchy

*Page 84:* ©Mallory Samson (bridal gown by Kirstie Kelly; bridesmaids' gowns by Kirstie Kelly)

*Page 85:* ©Julie Skarratt (bridal gown by Josephine Sasso; mother-of-the-bride gown by Josephine Sasso)

*Page 86:* ©Therese Marie Wagner

*Page 87:* ©Antonio M. Rosario (tiara from Paris Tiaras; handbag and antique gloves from private collection)

*Page 88:* ©Lyn Hughes

*Page 89:* ©Andrea Sperling

*Page 91:* ©Lyn Hughes

*Page 92:* ©Julie Skarratt (bridesmaid gown by Josephine Sasso)

*Page 94:* ©Antonio M. Rosario (boutonniere: Elizabeth Ryan; ballroom chair courtesy of TriServe Party Rentals; linens courtesy of Just Linens; tuxedo jacket from private collection)

*Page 95:* ©Jason Walz

*Page 97:* ©Lyn Hughes

*Page 98:* ©Antonio M. Rosario (baskets and floral design: Bette Matthews; wedding rings by George Sawyer, courtesy of The Clay Pot)

*Page 99:* ©Kit Latham

*Page 100:* ©Tanya Tribble

*Page 101:* ©Therese Marie Wagner

*Page 102:* ©Nancy Palubniak

*Page 103:* ©Andrea Sperling

*Page 104:* ©Antonio M. Rosario (floral design: Elizabeth Ryan; calligraphy: Bette Matthews; chairs, tables, dishes, place card holders, votives, and tableware courtesy of TriServe Party Rentals; linens courtesy of Just Linens)

*Page 105:* ©Karen Hill

*Page 106:* ©Therese Marie Wagner

*Page 107:* ©Therese Marie Wagner

*Page 108:* ©Antonio M. Rosario (calligraphy: Hilary Williams/Hil-Ink; tableware courtesy of TriServe Party Rentals; linens courtesy of Just Linens)

*Page 109:* ©Lyn Hughes

*Page 110:* ©Colleen Duffley (floral design: Two Design Group Events)

*Page 111:* ©Eliot Holtzman

*Page 113:* ©Paul Barnett

*Page 114:* ©Antonio M. Rosario (calligraphy: Susan L. Ramsey/Calligraphic Creations; bouquet: Bette Matthews; ballroom chair courtesy of TriServe Party Rentals; photographed at The Boathouse in Central Park)

*Page 115:* ©Antonio M. Rosario (floral design: Jennifer Pfeiffer/Magnolia; calligraphy: Angela R. Welch/Pen and Pauper; linens courtesy of the Cloth Connection; photographed at The Boathouse in Central Park)

*Page 117:* ©Jason Walz

*Page 118:* ©Jason Walz

*Page 121:* ©Jason Walz

*Page 123:* ©Roy Llera (cake by Ana Paz)

*Page 124:* ©Lyn Hughes

*Page 125:* ©Martin Jacobs

*Page 127:* ©Joshua Ets-Hokin

*Page 128–129:* ©Karen Hill

*Page 130:* ©Joshua Ets-Hokin

*Page 131:* ©Jason Walz

*Page 132:* ©Karen Hill

*Page 133:* ©Antonio M. Rosario (floral design: Bette Matthews; tablecloths courtesy of the Cloth Connection; tableware courtesy of TriServe Party Rentals; napkins courtesy of Just Linens; photographed at The Boathouse in Central Park)

*Page 134:* ©Andrea Sperling

*Page 135:* ©Antonio M. Rosario (floral design: Elizabeth Ryan; tables and tableware courtesy of TriServe Party Rentals; linens courtesy of Just Linens)

*Page 136:* ©Paul Barnett

*Page 137:* ©Antonio M. Rosario (floral design: Elizabeth Ryan; calligraphy: Stephannie Barba; dishes, napkin rings, votives, and tableware courtesy of TriServe Party Rentals; linens courtesy of Just Linens)

*Page 139:* ©Eliot Holtzman